TWAYNE'S WORLD AUTHORS SERIES

A Survey of the World's Literature

Sylvia E. Bowman, Indiana University

GENERAL EDITOR

POLAND

Adam Gillon, State University of New York College
at New Paltz

EDITOR

Maria Dabrowska

(TWAS 16)

TWAYNE'S WORLD AUTHOR'S SERIES (TWAS)

The purpose of TWAS is to survey the major writers —novelists, dramatists, historians, poets, philosophers, and critics—of the nations of the world. Among the national literatures covered are those of Australia, Canada, China, Eastern Europe, France, Germany, Greece, India, Italy, Japan, Latin America, New Zealand, Poland, Russia, Scandinavia, Spain, and the African nations, as well as Hebrew, Yiddish, and Latin Classical literatures. This survey is complemented by Twayne's United States Authors Series and English Authors Series.

The intent of each volume in these series is to present a critical-analytical study of the works of the writer; to include biographical and historical material that may be necessary for understanding, appreciation, and critical appraisal of the writer; and to present all material in clear, concise English—but not to vitiate the scholarly content of the work by doing so.

Maria Dabrowska

By Zbigniew Folejewski

University of Illinois

Twayne Publishers, Inc.   ::   New York

To the Memory of K. W. Zawodzinski
Poet, Critic, Scholar

Preface

In May of 1962, literary scholars, critics, and writers from Poland and many other countries paid tribute to Maria Dabrowska at the International Session of the Polish Academy held in Warsaw and in Kalisz, the ancient city near the writer's birthplace. That occasion marked the fiftieth anniversary of Maria Dabrowska's literary start and very nearly coincided with the seventieth anniversary of her life.

Maria Dabrowska is, if not the greatest, then certainly one of the greatest contemporary writers in Poland; her place in world literature is also secure, a place acknowledged not only by numerous translations of her works into foreign languages Eastern and Western, but by critics, both in Poland and abroad, who regard her as one of those few artists who have something important to say in the world of modern letters, as a contributor to the universal treasure of forms and ideas. It is quite natural that her name was considered by the Nobel Prize Committee, especially since her work is imbued with the universal human ideals so congenial to the last will of Alfred Nobel, the real meaning of which has recently come under renewed discussion in Sweden.

In spite of her literary stature, Maria Dabrowska's work has not yet had a definitive discussion even in Polish scholarly literature, and at least a concise introduction to her chief literary works in one of the major languages is badly needed. The present volume is an attempt to provide such a study.

In view of the limited scope of this series, the analysis of Dabrowska's work, too, is limited, the main stress being almost exclusively on her artistic narrative prose, i.e., on her short stories and novels. To assemble her dramatic works, literary criticism, and journalistic output would take many volumes. A thorough analysis of her work in each of these genres would certainly be a gratifying task; in the present volume, however, this material is only used to the extent that it is relevant to the discussion of the writer's stories and her tetralogy of *Nights and Days*.

This study consists of six chapters. Chapter One presents Dabrowska's intellectual background and literary heritage, her appearance on the literary scene, and her artistic development as manifested in her earlier volumes of short stories. In Chapters Two and Three, Dabrowska's main work as a novelist is discussed. She is placed in a wider context of contemporary trends in European literature, and the main features of her style are discussed. Chapter Four is devoted mainly to the postwar period, which marks Dabrowska's further development as an artist. A brief account of the reception of Dabrowska's work by literary critics is given in Chapter Five. The Conclusion, Chapter Six, must be somewhat tentative since we are dealing here with a living writer, and the impact of the fluctuating policies on literary art in her country during the last two decades still cannot be fully assessed. Nevertheless, the main aspects of Dabrowska's work will perhaps stand out clearly enough for the reader to form an opinion of this writer and her place in world literature.

Of course, one serious difficulty in presenting Dabrowska to an American audience is the fact that, so far, only a few of her works have been translated into English. For this reason the quotations in this volume, especially those characteristic of Dabrowska's views or—to the extent that this is possible in translation—of her style, are occasionally somewhat more extensive than would be necessary in the case of a prominent American writer.

During this author's visit to Poland in May, 1964, Maria Dabrowska, despite her failing health, granted him an interview in her home in Warsaw. It turned into a gracious and revealing literary conversation in which Dabrowska pointed out problems in her own writings and those of others which were of particular interest to her. She was most helpful in clarifying some biographical and literary details which will be reflected in the volume. It may be mentioned here that two questions in particular resulted in a longer and more animated discussion: the problem of the relationship between Dabrowska's work and the work of Joseph Conrad, and the problem of her relationship to Socialist

Realism, some aspects of which were termed by this author "a noble compromise." It should be stressed here that Dabrowska did not entirely agree with some of the remarks of this author, and that he himself bears sole responsibility for his views as finally formulated in this study.

I wish to gratefully acknowledge the financial help of the Graduate School of the University of Wisconsin for technical assistance in completing this book. I owe my thanks to my assistant, Mr. Lauren Leighton, who was very helpful in editing the manuscript and preparing the index and the bibliography. To Professor Adam Gillon and Professor Sylvia Bowman I wish to express my thanks for their patience in reading the manuscript and for their helpful suggestions. To Mr. Robert Milch my best thanks are due for his tedious and thorough copy-editing work, which has improved the presentation without causing a loss of identity of the author's style. Because this volume is addressed to the general reader in English-speaking countries, the author has complied with the publisher's wish to omit the diacritical marks used in the Polish language.

ZBIGNIEW FOLEJEWSKI

P. S. Just a few months after the completion of this work, a message from Warsaw reported that Maria Dabrowska died on May 19, 1965. May this modest study be a tribute to one of the great artists of our time.

Z. F.

June, 1965

Contents

Chronology

1889 Maria Szumska born on October 6 in Russow near the city of Kalisz. Father, Josef Szumski; mother, Ludomira, née Galczynska.

1901– School years in Kalisz as boarder in a private school of
1904 Mrs. Sedemani.

1905– Warsaw; enrolled in a private boarding school of Miss
1908 Havelke where several outstanding scholars were teachers; Polish literature was taught by Ignacy Chrzanowski, who later was Professor at the Jagellonian University in Cracow.

1908– University studies in Lausanne, Switzerland (Natural Sci-
1909 ence).

1909– Brussels, Belgium; continued university studies, lively par-
1912 ticipant in Polish émigré organizations; articles on cooperative movement, trade unions, educational ideas, etc. for Polish periodicals. Marriage with Marian Dabrowski, a Socialist political refugee after the revolution of 1905. Degree of "candidat ès sciences naturelles"; return to Poland, then journey to England to study the organization of consumers cooperatives.

1914 Publication of the story, "Little John" ("Janek") in the Warsaw weekly, *Prawda*, No. 23.

1914– Work as journalist for Polish newspapers and magazines,
1918 writing on economic, social, and political problems; a number of stories published.

1918– Husband dies. Civil service in Warsaw. Increasing literary
1925 activity. Several collections of short stories published.

1926 Great literary success of *People from Yonder* (*Ludzie stamtad*).

1928 *Liudi ottuda*, Russian translation of *People from Yonder*, published in Moscow.

1931   "A Talk with Friends" ("Rozmowa z przyjaciolmi") and "On a Difficult Road" ("Na ciezkiej drodze"): two articles in protest against the imprisonment of Polish political opposition leaders in the fortress of Brzesc by the Pilsudski government, published in *Wiadomosci Literackie* Nos. 3, 4.

1932   The first two volumes of the tetralogy, *Nights and Days* (*Noce i dnie*) appear in Warsaw; hailed by the critics as "the literary event of the day."

1933–   The rest of the cycle *Nights and Days* published. A 40-
1934   page-long study, "Maria Dabrowska: The Literary Significance of Her Work," ("Maria Dabrowska: historycznoliterackie znaczenie jej tworczosci") by Karol W. Zawodzinski, appears in *Przeglad Wspolczesny*. The author terms Dabrowska's accomplishment "epoch-making."

1936   "The Yearly Disgrace" ("Doroczny wstyd"), an article in *Dziennik Popularny,* No. 43, in protest against antisemitic action in Polish universities and against nationalistic excesses.

1937   *Crossroads* (*Rozdroze*), a book propagating more efficient land reform in Poland to improve the situation of millions of poor peasants.

1938   *Signs of Life* (*Znaki zycia*), a volume of stories. *Nächte und Täge*, German translation of the first two volumes of *Nights and Days,* published in Breslau.

1939   *The Orphan Genius* (*Geniusz sierocy*), Dabrowska's first dramatic work.

1939–   War period, mostly in Warsaw. Besides lecturing in under-
1945   ground educational organizations and daily struggle for survival, Dabrowska is working on a novel depicting life under the German occupation; parts of this unfinished novel were later published in Dabrowska's *Selected Works* in 1956. Also working on a Polish translation from English of *The Diary* of Samuel Pepys, subsequently published in 1952. After having survived the Warsaw Uprising and the destruction of the city by the Germans in 1944, Dabrowska walks out of Warsaw and finds temporary shelter in the country near Lowicz.

1945   Return to Warsaw (later related in the first part of *The Morning Star,* published in 1955).

Chronology

1945–1955	Years of silence; occasional attempts at critical reevaluation of Dabrowska's work from the position of Socialist Realism in its so-called Stalinist phase. Only one larger work by Dabrowska appeared during this period: a historical play set in the 11th century, *Stanislaw and Bogumil*, Warsaw, 1948.
1955	Publication of *The Morning Star* (*Gwiazda Zaranna*), a collection of stories from postwar Poland (some minor concessions for the principles of Socialist Realism but uncompromising stand on basic moral and artistic issues). *The Literary Art of Maria Dabrowska* (*Sztuka pisarska Marii Dabrowskiej*), the first book-length study of Dabrowska, by W. Maciag (following the critical line of Socialist Realism adepts on the point of ideological content, but praising the writer's artistic mastery). A new German translation of *Nights and Days* appears in Berlin.
1956	Publication of Dabrowska's *Selected Works* (*Pisma wybrane*) and of her lectures and articles from the "silent" period, *Thoughts of Problems and People* (*Mysli o sprawach i ludziach*).
1957	*Maria Dabrowska*, a collection of essays on Dabrowska and excerpts from her own comments on her work, edited by Z. Libera. *A Village Wedding and Other Stories*, English translation of *Gwiazda Zaranna*.
1959	Dabrowska's *Essays on Conrad* (*Szkice o Conradzie*) appears in book form. A Chinese translation of *Nights and Days* (*Hei-yeh-yü Pai-chou*) appears in Peiping.
1962	An International Symposium under the auspices of the Polish Academy, held in Warsaw and Kalisz in honor of Maria Dabrowska on the occasion of the 50th anniversary of her literary activity.
1963	The proceedings of the 1962 Symposium published, *Fifty Years of Maria Dabrowska's Creative Work*.
1964	*Nochi i dni*, Russian translation of *Nights and Days* published in Moscow.
1965	Maria Dabrowska dies in Warsaw on May 19th at the age of 75.

CHAPTER 1

Heritage, Apprenticeship, First Accomplishment: *The Cycle of* People from Yonder

> ". . . That bitter sense of freedom
> which comes of total deprivation."
> Albert Camus, *The Plague*

I *Heritage*

A S was mentioned in the Preface, the celebration of the fiftieth anniversary of Dabrowska's creative work coincided quite closely with her seventieth birthday. Maria Dabrowska, née Szumska, was born on October 6, 1889,[1] in the estate Russow near the city of Kalisz, in west-central Poland. Dabrowska's father, Joseph Dabrowski—like Bogumil, the hero of her novel—belonged to the pauperized gentry; he was no longer a landowner, but administered the estate of Russow. On the whole, many features of both the rural life in Russow and city life in Kalisz—transformed and fictionalized, of course (e.g., Kaliniec in her novel *Nights and Days*)—are incorporated in Dabrowska's literary works, the highly reminiscent character of which contributed to the general impression of authenticity.

Dabrowska's first more serious literary attempts date back to 1912 when she was a student just over twenty years old.[2] At that time Maria Dabrowska, like so many other Poles, studied abroad. Educational facilities in Poland, especially in the part that belonged to Russia, were very limited at that time and not easily accessible for Poles. They were even more inaccessible for women, especially in the field of natural sciences which Dabrowska, as her great compatriot Maria Sklodowska-Curie had done earlier, chose as her major field of study. Dabrowska spent a year (1908–1909) in Lausanne, Switzerland, and then went to Belgium where at the University of Brussels in the course of three years (1909–1912) she completed her program of study, passing the finals for the degree of "candidat ès sciences naturelles."

All this time she was also involved in very intense journalistic and patriotic activity in Polish émigré circles in Belgium. There she married Marian Dabrowski, a young historian who had been active in the socialist movement in Poland and had been forced to flee the country after the revolution of 1905. She gradually developed from an occasional correspondent to Polish periodials into an accomplished writer, critic, and translator. It was thus she experienced the same literary apprenticeship as her great predecessors in Polish literature, Henryk Sienkiewicz and Boleslaw Prus. From reporting facts she went on to the composition of smaller and then larger pieces in which life and fiction blend together in such a way that finally elements of fiction often look like reality, and reality acquires the proportions of artistically perfected vision; this attitude, from the early start, brought the author close to the ideal of realism as it was understood and practiced by the French masters.

The work which the writer herself regarded as her first literary achievement, and which she later included in her volume of stories, *The Smile of Childhood* (*Usmiech dziecinstwa,* Warsaw, 1923), was a story entitled "Little John" ("*Janek*"), submitted to the reputable Polish weekly *Prawda* (*Truth*) and published in its No. 23, 1914. At that time Dabrowska was already a well-established (and relatively well-paid) contributor to several periodicals. Speaking strictly chronologically, she was also the author of a couple of earlier published stories which, however, she did not regard worth mentioning as literary achievements. There is not much in this story that lets one anticipate the future author of one of the most important epic works in modern Polish literature. The "story" is actually, as the writer herself called it, "a remembrance," "a delightful picture of the world of a little country boy." And yet, there are in this brief plotless sketch some of the qualities which later will make Dabrowska's work so remarkable. These qualities include, first of all, the sharpness and freshness of observation, the ability of psychological penetration, which made it possible for the writer to show her readers a vision of the world as seen through the eyes of a child; finally, there is the simplicity and clarity of her style. These are probably the reasons why the author received the Publishers' Prize when she published this story, together with several others of similar character, in the volume, *The Smile of Childhood.*

"Little John" was well received, and the editor of *Prawda* who had accepted the story encouraged the young writer to go on with her creative work. This she did, courageously and somewhat naively blending impressions from life and undertaking more and more independent and accomplished literary compositions. The progressive groups in Poland with which Dabrowska was associated were very interested at that time in the cooperative movement flourishing in Western Europe, in Belgium, England, and the Scandinavian countries. Dabrowska was early attracted to this movement and for many years became an active member and worker propagating cooperatives as the best solution for the notorious poverty of the Polish peasant masses. Besides numerous articles she produced a book-form account, *Finland, The Model Country of Cooperatives* (*Finlandia, wzorowy kraj kooperacji,* Warsaw, 1913), and *Cooperatives in Belgian Villages* (*Kooperatywy na wsi belgijskiej,* Warsaw, 1913). A considerable part of her literary production of that time propagates the idea of cooperatives as almost a panacea for various economic and social problems. The young writer was very definitely under the influence of those foreign and Polish circles which believed that most political and economic problems could be solved by gradual reforms based on the principle of cooperatives. These notes can also be heard in Dabrowska's literary writings, for example in such stories as "Alex" ("Olek"),[3] a somewhat didactic presentation of the beneficial results of cooperative ideas among youngsters, or "The Misery of Wheat" ("Niedola pszenicy"), in which Dabrowska alludes to the "miraculous power" hidden in people if they know how to use it for the common good, while otherwise, if it serves an egoistic purpose, the greatest treasure (in this case, wheat being hoarded for speculation) can be a curse. This, incidentally, reminds one somewhat of the symbolism of the treasure in Conrad's *Nostromo,* although at that time[4] Dabrowska perhaps did not even know that novel. Her knowledge of English was quite limited before her stay in England in 1912–1913, and *Nostromo* was first translated into Polish in 1928. It is rather an early evidence of a certain moral and artistic affinity which will often be noticeable in Dabrowska's later development and her frequent discussions of Conrad's work.

On the whole, the stories which Dabrowska selected for the volume *The Branch of a Cherry Tree* (*Galez czeresni*) mark a distinct shift toward a more serious and conscious vision of the reality in which not everything is as "smiling," idyllic, as in the volume *The Smile of Childhood*. Incidentally, the chronology here may seem misleading; *The Smile of Childhood* was published a year after *The Branch of a Cherry Tree,* but most of the stories in the later volume were written somewhat earlier. Their prevailing "sunny" character was explained by the fact that they were written largely for a magazine for children called *In the Sun* (*W sloncu*). "It was a challenging title in view of the cloudy reality," said Dabrowska in her essay "Warsaw of My Youth." "I, too, had this spirit of challenge in me. I was interested not in what was impossible to do in these conditions, but in what one could do in spite of these bad conditions that would be good and that would make the bright future closer or at least make one believe that it is possible." [5]

II *Apprenticeship and Success*

In Polish literature there had been a well-established tradition of art serving the national "cause." This was so during the period of Romanticism which ended in Messianism, and it was so during the period of Realism, when Polish writers felt that they should describe constructive "positive" elements of daily life so as to teach their society to build up a better life "from foundations." The young Dabrowska follows this tradition both in her social and professional activity and in her literary works in which she tries to promote progress, education, cooperation, faith in the future, faith in humanity. This optimism, this faith, however, does not overshadow her sense of reality and her keen feeling for the tragic elements in human life. The nineteenth-century Polish woman writer, Eliza Orzeszkowa, has clearly been one of her teachers,[6] but at the same time there is a strong affinity with the more modern and even modernistic method of Stefan Zeromski in the perfection of psychological motivation of individual and collective decisions. With Zeromski, Dabrowska shares an interest in idealistic socialism, her faith in the ability of people to improve their collective existence without the misery and terror so often associated with social revolutions. This explains why Dabrowska devoted her youth to the cooperative movement, serving and propagating its cause in an attempt to combine her idea of social usefulness with a strictly artistic interest in human beings, in their fate as individuals and as members of a collective.

In one of her early articles on cooperatives in Belgium, Maria Dabrowska used as a motto the optimistic slogan formulated by the Polish philosopher and social leader, Edward Abramowski. Abramowski spoke of the cooperative movement as making possible "moral transformation of slaves into free, life-shaping human beings." Apparently this idea appealed not only to Dabrowska's social convictions but also to her artistic imagination. The phenomenon of such a transformation can be found in the souls of her later literary heroes in a number of stories—especially in the cycle, *People from Yonder*—sometimes even in situations where basic conditions for any real social change, conditions which would seem necessary to justify such a process, were all but nonexistent. What we face here is the problem of Dabrowska's slowly crystallizing poetics, in which the concept of psychologically true vision more and more replaces the naturalistic requirement of socially faithful presentation of reality. Apart from certain analogies with the Polish writer Stefan Zeromski, the main artistic force in this process was Dabrowska's contact and fascination with Scandinavian literature. At the turn of the century, at the time when Western Europe and America were still "discovering" Russian realism, Scandinavian literature penetrated into Poland and Russia leaving an imprint, especially on drama. In her memoirs Dabrowska noted strong impressions from such plays as Ibsen's *Nora,* and in her novel *Nights and Days* there are passages devoted to the intriguing "satanic" figure of Stanislaw Przybyszewski. By way of personal contact with Scandinavian artists and his writing and editorial work in the periodical *Zycie,* as well as through his lectures and speeches, Przybyszewski spread the fame of Scandinavian literature in Poland and Russia.[7]

One of the direct manifestations of Dabrowska's interest in Scandinavian literatures was her translation of a novel by the Danish writer Jens Peter Jacobsen, *Niels Lyhne* (written in 1880).

Dabrowska's translation was published in Warsaw in 1927. In an article on problems of literary translation, "A Few Thoughts on Translation Work" ("Pare mysli o pracy przekladowej", *Tworczosc*, 1954), Dabrowska described in some detail how she went through a laborious process of translating this Danish novel, first indirectly from a German translation and then comparing the Polish text sentence by sentence with the Danish original, not knowing Danish and depending almost entirely on its similarity to German with only slight outside help. She stresses the fact that one of the reasons for the youthful enthusiasm with which she undertook this task, and which enabled her to endure its tedious procedure, was the fact that *Niels Lyhne* was "one of the most cherished novels of her youth." In Dabrowska's introduction to the work we find several remarks which throw a certain light on her artistic convictions and inclinations. Especially characteristic is her emphasis on the Danish writer's "love for the mysteries of human life," which in her opinion constitutes one of the most important qualities of Jacobsen's work. At that time Dabrowska was the author of the collection *People from Yonder*, (*Ludzie stamtad*, Warsaw, 1926) and it is quite easy to see in these stories the same quality of concern, love, understanding for everyday events in the lives of ordinary people with their ordinary thoughts and feelings, passions and doubts, sins and sacrifices.

Her statement about the secret of Jacobsen's talent can certainly be applied to her own. One can go even further. The above formula of "love for the mysteries of human life" may constitute a key to a better understanding of her approach to the world, depicted in her *People from Yonder*. Dabrowska describes here the world of the landless agricultural proletariat, farm laborers, migratory workers, squatters, tramps. In an attempt to penetrate the mysteries of their inner life, she sometimes resorts to the device of "transformation"; she lets her uneducated, illiterate individuals express their thoughts in terms that are quite beyond their social level and education. From the point of view of a formal, literal interpretation of realism, certain reservations of some critics are perhaps justified. However, Dabrowska is quite convincing in her preface to the second edition of the volume, where she defends this seemingly excessive "poetization" by pointing out that, even viewed from the strictly social point of view, it can be motivated by a natural and perfectly understandable urge, present in any human being, to break out of the actual limits of existence. Recognizing the fact that "transformation" is impossible on purely social grounds, the author shifts it to another, "metaphysical" dimension. This subjective method of Dabrowska, as those of many other twentieth-century writers, breaks with the practice of "pure" realism.

Nevertheless, the collection *People from Yonder* can be treated as a highly realistic presentation of the farm laborer's world. This by itself was a novel and important phenomenon in the history of Polish literature which, being traditionally a literature of the gentry, had rather neglected the life of the lower social classes. It is true that a certain interest in the life of peasants is present both in the writing of Romantic poets and during the period of Realism, but, of course, the approach there was quite different. For both the Romantic and post-Romantic artists, the vision of peasant life was highly idealized; so much, in fact, that in some works of Julius Slowacki, for example, the peasant element in Polish life, viewed in historical perspective, became the symbol of the peaceful "angelic" element as opposed to the gentry element, which symbolized the spirit of progress, to be sure, but progress by constant, violent struggle.

Speaking much later of her work on the novel *Nights and Days,* which depicts rural life in Poland, though not the life of peasants, Dabrowska recalls one of Joseph I. Kraszewski's novels, *The Hut on the Outskirts of the Village (Chata za wsia)* as a "family novel," well-written and thematically close to her heart. Joseph I. Kraszewski (1812–1877) was one of the first writers in Polish literature to describe the life of the peasant with a measure of realism. Still, Kraszewski's concept of the peasant is basically Romantic, even pre-Romantic, one could say, since there is a great deal of sentimentalism in his portrayal of the peasant's hard life, which evokes the sympathy of the reader without going to the bottom of the social problem involved. Thus, in his peasant novels we have either a pretty, good girl seduced by a rich land-owner (e.g., *Ulana, The Guard, The Story of Sawko*) or else a good, gifted peasant boy (e.g., *Ostap Bondarczuk*) in love with the landlord's daughter, whose love he wins but not happiness because of his low social standing. Despite Kraszewski's considerable realism in the presentation of various details of peasant life, he observes the described reality as if he were watching a fascinating exotic show from the porch of a mansion. The reader is supposed to be moved by the "innocent beauty" and the individual tragedy of these heroes, but the general tone and especially the black and white coloring is too conventional.

During the period of Realism the image of the peasant under went a considerable change. Eliza Orzeszkowa, Boleslaw Prus, and Adolf Dygasinski portrayed the life of Polish peasants in a number of stories and novels in which the idealized, moving peasant heroes and heroines are no longer literary "types," but fully developed characters. Even in such excellent novels as *The Outpost* by Prus or *Dziurdziowie* by Orzeszkowa, a certain amount of didacticism is still present, but at least the peasants live independent lives; their victories and defeats are plausible since the peasants are neither good angels nor evil monsters, as they sometimes were portrayed during the period of Romanticism.

At the turn of the century W. S. Reymont wrote his immense four-volume peasant novel *The Peasants* (*Chlopi*), which became the classic work of its kind in Polish literature. However, Reymont, like his predecessors, speaks almost exclusively of peasant-farmers, people of some means and some social rights. Polish literature at that time had nothing like Ivan Turgenev's *Hunter's Sketches,* in which the writer shows a surprising insight into both peasant psychology and into the social conditions of the peasant class. Except for a few stories by Stefan Zeromski, the only important work in Poland devoted to the life of the landless farm proletariat was the novel *Komornicy* (*The Squatters*) by W. Orkan (1900).

Dabrowska, like Turgenev in Russia, took up the theme of landless peasants mainly as an artistic motif, and not as a purely social problem. But as in Turgenev's case, Dabrowska's volume was often discussed as a work of political nature, and some critics discussed its merits and demerits in this light. Considering Dabrowska's involvement in professional and social organizations with some political affiliations, this confusion of Dabrowska the agitator and Dabrowska the writer is not surprising. Incidentally, the first review of one of her literary works (*The Branch of the Cherry*

Tree) appeared in the leftist biweekly *Kultura Robotnicza* (*Working Class Culture*), No. 13, 1922.

However, the publication of *People from Yonder* made it obvious that the author did not resort to fiction in order to propagate political slogans, but to express her deep interest in the lives of the people she had observed closely during her childhood in Russow. There was an element of true epic in this attempt to capture a certain form of life at the moment when it was already disappearing. The Poland of larger and smaller estates was gradually changing into a more modern country, and the people connected with the old pattern of rural life portrayed in this volume—all these "farm-hands, night-watchmen, shepherds, milkmaids and charwomen" whom Dabrowska regards as "the last people in the world"—were becoming almost non-existent as a typical group because of the exodus to industrial cities. In Dabrowska's book, they are brought back to life, and their simple, almost biological existence strikes one as fully human. Dabrowska's artistic vision caught them, as she said in an interview in the weekly, *Wiadomosci Literackie,* "in difficult moments of their lives."

III *The World of* People from Yonder

It was said that the volume *People from Yonder* made the young author famous, and decided her entire career. Indeed, she became an acknowledged writer almost overnight, greeted almost unanimously by the reviewers as a new big name. Even where there were reservations, Dabrowska's keen sense of observation and the purity and simplicity of her language and style were acknowledged. Not all of the critics who regarded *People from Yonder* as a minor work, wondering whether Dabrowska would ever equal W. S. Reymont's huge fresco, *The Peasants,* were aware of the fact that in this seemingly loosely assembled collection of stories there was from the beginning a well-balanced and artistically motivated unity of structure. It is here, in this first notion of a larger unit, of an artistic synthesis developing out of earlier fragmentary efforts, that the actual breakthrough took place in Dabrowska's career. And speaking of this unity, it must be stressed that it is not only the unity of social and topographic milieu and the unity of realistic method in its re-creation; there is also a clear line of composition in which the seemingly separate stories serve the function of traditional chapters in a novel. Consequently there is an interesting interplay of two technical devices: Each of the stories follows, of course, the basic principles of short-story technique, such as the unity and uniqueness of motif, setting, and mood, and the significance of final effect. However, at the same time, each of these separate units is subordinated to the structural principles of a larger unit which in this case resembles the form of a traditional novel. One could point out the particular novelistic form, namely that of Zola's *La terre* or Reymont's *The Peasants,* as being constructed on similar, almost biological principles of the natural course in nature and in the life of people close to nature. The course of this natural biological process in Dabrowska's volume described an almost full circle, the main difference from the above-mentioned novels lying in the fact that in *People from Yonder,* the vision of human life goes beyond the concept of naturalism, especially obvious in Zola's work, but also present in Reymont. The emphasis in Dabrowska's work is shifted from the biological and materialistic ground to the psychological and moral sphere.

Dabrowska herself describes somewhat poetically the composition of *People from Yonder* in the preface to the second edition of the book in 1935 in the following words:

Independently of the dramatic plot of each story, the theme as a whole begins with a dawn, the interplay of youthful instincts ("The Wild Plant") which, after having gone through the stage of increasing passions and self-indulgences (Lucia and Peter), culminating in moments of pain and doubt (Nicodemus and Wityk), begins to rise gradually from the prayer of a beggar through the triumph of Dionysius and through the courage of little Julia ("The Longest Road") and a kind of consolation. And in the last story ("The Cuckoo-Clock") the theme ends with the evening image of the old age and death of the priest-healer as the only form in which the primitive providence stepped down to these people.

The first story, "The Wild Plant" ("Dzikie ziele") is indeed a kind of a serene idyllic preamble. Again Turgenev comes to mind as we perceive this finely drawn "sketch," faithful and realistic in detail and yet romantic in its somewhat dreamy mood of the village landscape as a background to the deep, almost violent, passion of the simple servant girl, Marynka, and a farm hand. There is, to be sure, a certain amount of naturalism in the description of the erotic urge and its almost animal fulfillment, but at the same time there is the final sublimation of these emotions and then their sanctioning by a wedding and subsequent marital happiness. Though the moral is quite conventional, it is not trite in its final effect, so convincing is the development of the gradual elevation of the couple's passionate love and their ability to find community in hard labor and attachment to land not even their own.

The next stories bring the growing tension between the conventional concept of idyllic peasant life and the reality of poverty, hunger, sicknesses, constant worry, minor and major transgressions of criminal and moral laws, all quite typical and yet unique in that the writer is able to outline in each individual case a truthful and convincing situation and directly or indirectly to dramatize the full psychological motivation of this or that behavior on the part of her unheroic heroes.

The stories "Lucia from Pukucice" ("Lucja z Pokucic") and "Glass Horses" ("Szklane konie") are constructed on the traditional principle of human nature as weak and erratic, but, nevertheless, human. Lucia, daughter of well-to-do peasants, who married a farm hand, experiences a feeling of emptiness when her husband is inducted into the Russian army and then taken prisoner by the Japanese. There is a masterful analysis of Lucia's small everyday problems and worries which somehow, unintentionally, bring her together with another man and then still another—until she finds herself almost an outcast in the "public opinion" of the village. There is still no real tragedy here, but the carefree optimism of Marynka from the previous story gives way to a note of loneliness and moral confusion. In these perfectly natural and deeply human situations there is a note of the sadness of existence, a note so often heard in Scandinavian literature. A similar note of awareness of unavoidable failings and sufferings in human life constitutes the main motif of the next story, "Glass Horses." In the same way that Lucia cannot change the course of her relationship to men, so is Peter unable to stop drinking, falling deeper and deeper into the habit and into difficulties in his work.

The climax of the tragic course comes in the story "Night over the World" ("Noc ponad swiatem"), where we have the portrait of a human wreck—a man slowly, limb by limb, destroyed by syphilis, a man who realizes that any pity he can draw from others will always be mixed with abhorrence. When the only living creature that does not panic at the sight of him—his dog, Lord—dies, nothing is left to keep him going. The story ends with a somber vision of day turning into night for this man who is so completely separated from any community with other human beings. Again we have the motif of loneliness as one of the most crucial problems in human life. "I am a man, too" is the last challenge of the man excluded by cruel fate from the human race, deprived even of his dog-friend. Being so completely, absolutely alone is simply not endurable for man.

The next story, "Consolation" ("Pocieszenie"), which culminates in the scene of the real death of a village shepherd, Wityk, is almost idyllic in its peaceful acceptance of fate. It is about the quiet, dignified death of a man who has fulfilled his modest duty, and who is missed by everybody. Thus the story forms a counterbalance to the previous tragic vision of living death. In the structure of the whole it constitutes almost an anticlimax.

But the real counterbalance and the thematically highest point in the volume is the story "The Triumph of Dionysius" ("Tryumf Dionizego"). This story, more than any other in the volume, contains the author's message. The culmination point—Dionysius' conversation with the village pariah—is an affirmation of life as an eternal synthesis of suffering and hope.

IV Miracle of Transformation

As was pointed out, in her outlook on the problems of life and death, the Polish author has an affinity with Scandinavian writers. However, both in her approach to the matter of physical death and to the matter of moral, spiritual death, when all the hopes of a man are smashed by fate, the Polish writer takes a somewhat different position, especially in comparison with those Scandinavian writers who represented the school of naturalism. It would be interesting to make a closer study of the scenes of death in such works as, for example, Zola's *La terre* and Jens Peter Jacobsen's *Niels Lyhne,* and to compare them with Dabrowska's. And in connection with this, the treatment of the problem of man's loneliness in the face of death throws additional light on Dabrowska's independent stand. Zola's purely naturalistic, biological treatment of these matters is partly overcome in Jacobsen's novel where the notion of human responsibility is put on a higher level. But Dabrowska goes still further in this direction. In spite of her high praise for Jacobsen's mastery as demonstrated by his penetrating vision of human fate, the Polish writer apparently felt the need to oppose his somewhat one-sided pessimistic conclusions in *Niels Lyhne*. Her thesis of the possibility of transformation of even the most tragic elements in human life into something positive, her affirmation of life as a synthesis of suffering and hope, her faith in the community of human beings even in the depths of social and moral degradation—all this seems a kind of protest against Jacobsen's pessimistic concept of man's absolute isolation on the way toward death. In this respect Dabrowska's attitude is closer to that of Joseph Conrad. In her essay on "Social and Religious Elements in Conrad," published in the Polish weekly *Wiadomosci Literackie* in 1932, Dabrowska made a direct reference to this problem, stating that in Conrad's work, notwithstanding his pessimism and his feeling of loneliness of man in the face of both life and death (she quotes *Heart of Darkness:* "We die as we dream —alone"), there are at the same time elements of struggle against this feeling, there is "longing for community of man with humanity and even more than humanity." "I confess [says Dabrowska] that to me personally this aspect of Conrad is more significant and important, since this is closer to my heart." [8]

In Jens Peter Jacobsen's novel *Niels Lyhne* there is a passage characteristic of the above mentioned problems. It refers to Niels Lyhne's thoughts at the moment of facing death:

When he thought of people, his spirit fell. He evoked them out of his memory, one after another, and they all passed by and left him alone, and not one would stop and stay with him . . .

The sad truth is that the human soul is always alone. It is all a lie about the community of one man's soul with another.[9]

All this is radically different from Dabrowska's message in *People from Yonder*. The hero of the story "The Triumph of Dionysius" would actually have much more reason for pessimism, but nevertheless finds a more affirmative answer. The tragic element seldom appears in Dabrowska's work in its "pure" classical form. Very rarely does she strike the note of, say, Conrad's "End of the Tether," or Zeromski's *Crows Will Hack Us to Pieces* (*Rozdziobia nas kruki, wrony*). In Dabrowska's work the tragic element is almost always (with the exception of "Night Over the World") counterbalanced by a note of hope and optimism, even in situations where it would seem impossible to find any room for it. The writer's faith in the power of simple human instinct toward decency and dignity even at the very bottom of life defies the most horrible situations.

Dionysius, the primitive, uneducated milkman-hero in the story, "The Triumph of Dionysius," expresses some of these thoughts in his discourse with Satan, the former villain and now village outcast who does not have anybody in the world who would care, anybody who would have anything else for him except disgust and . . . fear. To this man who has lost all hope in the world, the poor milkman, who himself, struck by a sudden sickness, could despair and rebel against life, starts explaining his thoughts, thoughts that are surprising even to himself, thoughts that he finds in a moment of revelation, only because of the need to help another human being, still more miserable and lonely than he is:

. . . The thing is that when one loses all the hopes, then for the first time he can see that he actually had not lost anything, for the hopes of other people enter his heart. For it is possible to live with what is the property of others. One can lose everything in the world and still have enough left, for your life is in everything . . . in every other human being . . . well, isn't it?

Satan did not listen. And Dionysius went on, silently now, with his thoughts on how joy and sorrow always follow each other. You must experience the one, whether you have any hopes or not, and you cannot escape the other no matter how you try. Your life and your salvation consist of them both.

No use trying to escape from anything. Just live, live with all your power. Even if you don't have anything with which to face catastrophe, meet it with nothing except your courage and your human heart.

There is something shining and important in you, something that can still be of some use for God, something that will go on fighting and will bring you unexpected triumphs.

"Triumphs of the Heavenly Lord." Just as it is in the Holy Song for today[10] so it should be in every man—now again speaking aloud, announced Dionysius.

Dazzled, he stumbled over a small stone and at once all these thoughts got entangled. He would not be capable of conceiving such thoughts again, not to speak of expressing them in words.[11]

All of this may seem too philosophical, too sophisticated for an uneducated milk-wagon driver. Indeed, as was mentioned before, there were critics who thought that Dabrowska spoiled the suggestiveness of her vision by letting these simple heroes express too many of her own ideas without sufficient regard for their intellectual limit. As to that, on the one hand we must remember that her argument in defense of her theory of "transformation" has some validity, and, on the other, we must point out that through a very skillful stylistic arrangment the writer succeeded in putting these reflective elements in such a context that they appear motivated to a high degree in spite of their somewhat too sophisticated character.

In the first place, it is a climactic point in the composition of the story, it is a rare, unique moment of sudden, almost miraculous revelation, "dazzlement," surprising to the hero himself. This completely unique character of the moment is indicated in the very title, being termed as a moment of a spiritual "triumph," a moment in which this man is able to "think and express" human truths that are normally beyond his comprehension. This is further emphasized—to make the situation psychologically more probable—by the remark that when Dionysius "stumbled over a small stone . . . at once all these thoughts got entangled. He would not have been capable of conceiving such thoughts again, not to speak of expressing them in words."

The general impression of authenticity both in this scene and throughout the book is intensified by the quite consistent stylization of the language. Dabrowska's concept of style here is based on the compromise between local dialect and standard language. In her narrative passages she uses literary language, simple, close to colloquial, with only a very limited admixture of poetization. Peasant dialect elements are discreetly and skillfully interwoven in the main stream of narration while in dialogues they are used quite freely so that the general impression is that the people speak their native dialect even though the general character is sufficiently close to standard language so as not to be any obstacle for the educated reader.

V *Forging the Style*

The question of bridging the gap between these two areas of expression—standard language and dialects—has been a serious problem in literature ever since it became clear that language in a work of art has its specific artistic function different from the strictly communicative function of language in actual life. During the period of Realism, the growing stress on the authenticity, or perhaps more exactly speaking, the impression of authenticity in a work of art brought attempts to make the various people speak in literary works as they would in actual life. However, since at the same time a work of art must appeal to the largest possible audience, a compromise usually was necessary in which all the features which were too distant from the national standard had to undergo a process of stylization. At the same time, owing to the strictly artistic "law" of internal unity of style, the language of the people depicted in the work would often influence the strictly narrative parts; especially with the increasing use of dialogues, their characteristic features were becoming more and more aggressive. Besides, in describing a given reality, a given geographic or social milieu, a number of its features could only be talked about with the reproduction of certain characteristic words, expressions, and even phonological peculiarities by which the described world was commonly known.[12]

Some writers would still insist that the work describing, for example, the life of the peasants from a certain region should be written in the authentic dialect of this region, but such experiments (as the novel *Marcyna* by J. Kedziora in Polish literature) had to remain outside of the main stream of national art.

Dabrowska's approach to these questions is that of moderation. She uses quite freely the authentic language of the peasants from her native province (which she knew very well indeed), but they are skillfully blended with elements of the literary language. The different systems are harmonized in most cases to such a degree that there is hardly any noticeable tension between them. This ability of "hiding" the artistic qualities constitutes one of the main achievements of Dabrowska as a stylist. The dialectal material is interwoven in the main stream of narrative parts and it is, of course, present in dialogues where the protagonists are uneducated country people, with certain distinctions between them, depending on their generation, position, etc. In this way the stories acquire not only *couleur local* but internally there is also the imprint of individual and social authenticity.

In general the style of the stories is simple and clear, adequate for the subject and understandable for all readers independently of the degree of their acquaintance with dialects. In the process of arranging the main structural elements, i.e., the dialogues and the narrative parts, Dabrowska quite frequently resorts to the device of the so-called *style indirect libre* or "reported speech," a device connected with the modern method of writing known as "stream of consciousness." In these parts, dialogue and monologue almost imperceptibly transfer into narration, still retaining certain features of direct speech. A good example of this form is the quoted discourse between Dionysius and Satan where there is no clear demarcation line between direct and indirect speech. There are many other examples of this device, usually in parts where the author relates animated conversation or a violent stream of recollections, as if there was no time for their complete stylistic transformation.

They reminded her that she, a daughter of landed peasants, would not marry as they wished. Then she took a tramp . . . . She did as she wanted, let her have it then . . . . They will help her now, all right, but let her not beg any more, and think that she has anything coming. For she was a bad daughter. Yes. Bad daughter.

Anything coming? Lucia did not come for that. She came to see if there was still any kind of life for her. If she is to hear a lot of criticism of the one that is in the war, and perhaps never will see the world, then she may just as well leave at once. ("Lucja from Pokucice") [13]

In the process of harmonizing the realistically reproduced elements of local dialect with the descriptive literary style there are, of course, certain inconsistencies, both in using dialect form and in poetization of narrative parts. However, these instances are not numerous and the inadequacies are not drastic. So, for example, one observes even in the quoted conversation between Dionysius and Satan how the third person singular of the auxiliary verb varies in its form in the speech of the same person (Polish dialectal je and jes besides the literary jest,[14] or the highly literary contracted pronoun form swe instead of the colloquial swoje), but the general character of the speech is not really spoiled by this.

Likewise, the author's lyrical digressions occasionally clash with the realistic context where she seems slavishly to follow the poetic style of the Young Poland period:

It was as he were not sitting on the cart, but as if he were in the aroma of alfalfa, and in the glittering water in the ditch . . . as if he were a hillock rising toward the clouds and then flying back to himself . . . . ("The Triumph of Dionysius")

It would be pedantry to make an issue of these rather rare instances where the blending of styles is not perfect. The important thing is that the general tone of Dabrowska's prose in this volume is highly uniform and strikes a note of authenticity and suggestiveness. The people, the situations in which they are found and their behavior in these situations, all this makes a distinct impression of reality. The "heroes" of the stories are neither the idealized "angelic souls" of the Romanticists, nor the "fabulously colorful" figures of the Young Poland, nor even the often somewhat didactically portrayed victims of social injustice of the realists; they are simple living people, people whose emotional and moral problems are quite ordinary and, therefore, deeply human. And this is the main reason why the volume People from Yonder enjoyed such a lively response to its first appearance, why it was greeted both by critics and by readers as an important event in Polish literature.

The Polish critic Karol W. Zawodzinski even went so far in his high praise of People from Yonder as to express the opinion that, "from the point of view of artistic structure and balance between the various elements, People from Yonder is the most perfect work in the entire production of the author of Nights and Days." [15]

To gain a better idea of the extent to which the volume really presents itself as a uniform "artistic structure," it is important to realize that the interplay between the various composing elements in separate stories, when seen as juxtapositions, show themselves almost as "situation rhymes" in the structure as a whole. There is, for example, such a beautiful formal, and at the same time symbolic, manifestation of this internal unity of composition in the contrasting endings of the three stories, "Night over the World," "Consolation," and "The Triumph of Dionysius." The first one ends with the vision of complete darkness, "night" falling over the world for the unfortunate hero barred from human community with his village. In the next story, the final note is that of hope and optimism. In spite of the fact that the subject here is the actual death of the old shepherd, Wityk, its symbolism is presented in the words of the village beggar who, wandering through the fields immediately after the funeral, cannot help expressing his praise of life:

A beautiful summer—he said—Thank God that it arrived; Thank God. Thank God.[16]

And as a direct echo of the vision of "night over the world," the story "The Triumph of Dionysius" ends with the opposite vision of the night which after the discourse between Dionysius and Satan is bright with hopeful light:

The sky was so bright that it seemed light blue. The indistinctly outlined fields were submerged not in darkness but in stars, and the moon gilded the wide spaces.[17]

Not only do we have references throughout the volume to the earlier stories, but sometimes a certain thread interrupted in one story will be taken up and carried further in another. So, for example, the final fate of Nicodemus from the story, "Night over the World" is related in the story. "The Cuckoo Clock" as a direct follow-up to the moment where the previous story ended; a dramatic scene is recalled in which the cursed man starts digging a grave for himself, and the subsequent events from his life are briefly narrated.

One can wonder whether Dabrowska's critics—or for that matter even she herself—fully realized the quite singular artistic significance of her achievment in creating a volume of short stories with such a degree of organic unity of composition. The accom-

plishment is quite unusual not only in the history of Polish literature but in the entire realm of world literature. It constitutes an
interesting and valuable contribution in this respect. The subject
as such has been discussed in various literatures, and various short-
story collections from Ivan Turgenev's *Hunter's Sketches* to Sher-
wood Anderson's *Winesburg, Ohio* have been mentioned as more
or less successful examples of short-story cycles characterized by
the unity of time and setting. But the purposefulness and the degree of internal unity of artistic composition of the whole in
Dabrowska's *People from Yonder* is hardly encountered in any
literature.

CHAPTER 2

Nights and Days: *Literary And Ideological Concept And Context*

> "The life that this ring had bound her to, that she complained about, angrily protested and revolted against and tried to tear apart—nevertheless she loved it so, joyed in it so, both in good times and bad, that there was not a single day which would not seem hard to give back to God, not one grief which she would have foregone without having missed it."
>
> Sigrid Undset, *Kristin Lavransdatter*

I *The Road to the Epic*

IT was mentioned in the preceding chapter that the so-called "little form," the short-story form, from the very beginning seems to have been insufficient for Dabrowska's talent, and that the volume, *People from Yonder,* had certain potential features of larger structure. This, of course, has nothing to do with any gradation of literary genres, i.e., with ascribing the novel form a greater artistic value and significance than the short-story form. Each one of these forms has its own autonomous artistic laws, its internal dynamics, and within each of these forms one can speak of greater or lesser degrees of artistic perfection.

As is well known, some of the greatest masters of world literature achieved their fame mainly as short-story writers, and some of the greatest among them, like Guy de Maupassant, Edgar Allan Poe, or Anton Chekhov, had never, or almost never, practiced the novel form. There are, of course, writers—Leo Tolstoy, Fyodor Dostoevsky, Henryk Sienkiewicz, etc.—who are known to the world as novelists par excellence, and who, at the same time, were able to express themselves with equal perfection in the short story form. There are those, too, with whom certain basic features of one or the other genre remain predominant even though they practice several genres; Joseph Conrad, for example, is predominantly a novel writer, and the novelistic technique is observable even in his shortest stories. As Ford Madox Ford stated, in an exaggerated but quite justified remark, Conrad never wrote "a true short story, a matter of two or three pages of minutely considered words, ending with a smack, with what the French call a *coup de canon*." [1]

Finally, there exist in contempory literatures manifestations of more or less total protest against any of the conventional patterns of the established literary genres, especially the genre of the novel. Actually, roots of such protests go quite far back into the past. In Polish literature Cyprian K. Norwid launched a vigorous attack in the second half of the nineteenth century against the conventional concept of both the novel and the short story; Norwid's reaction against the "terror of literary genre convention" was somewhat similar to contemporary experiments in creating something so completely different from the formal point of view that it would make the impression of "anti-novel" or "anti-short story." [2]

In the case of Maria Dabrowska, the situation is somewhat similar to that of Joseph Conrad. Only very rarely in her work do there appear stories which can be called "true short stories," i.e., stories with the tight economic plot rapidly gravitating toward a dramatic outcome, toward this *coup de canon*, with the speed of "a projectile ejected from a plane" and heading straight downward in distinction to the novelistic parabola of a projectile shot from the ground. [3] Not particularly interested in sheer formal experimentation, Dabrowska is not afraid of literary conventions and within this acceptance of the existing literary forms it was a natural and logical course which led this writer, with her ability to grasp the process of individual and collective life in its full meaning and dynamism, from the short story form toward the larger structure, the novel form. On the other hand, this larger structure which came after the cycle of *People from Yonder* is also in a way a cycle of stories, a chronicle of life not of a family or even a class, but of a whole period of collective Polish history, of the nights and days of several generations, representing a transition from one social structure to another and from one political form to another, from one ideology to one seemingly different, yet still the same from the point of view of the unchangeable ideals of human love, duty, and dignity.

[38]

Nights and Days

When Maria Dabrowska came out with the first volume of her novel, *Nights and Days,* literature in Poland and in Europe was still mainly characterized by the method of Realism, although James Joyce and Marcel Proust were achieving completely new dimensions in the process of re-creating life from memories and expressing the inner reality (the Polish translation of Proust's *A la recherche du temps perdu* appeared at that time), and William Faulkner's *Sanctuary* shocked readers with its bold deformation of "outer" reality. In Poland the boldest experiments in the field of expressionism and psychological realism were undertaken by Stanislaw I. Witkiewicz in the novel *The Parting with the Autumn* (*Pozegnanie z jesienia,* 1927) and by Karol Irzykowski in his *Paluba* (1903; *sic!*). At the same time, in the Soviet Union there developed the principles of socialist realism, containing some new approaches to the old problem of depicting reality from a given, strictly prescribed angle. Michael Sholokhov's novel, *Virgin Soil Upturned,* is a positive example of such an approach.

As was pointed out, Dabrowska is not particularly interested in strictly formal experiments in prose. Her short stories are quite conventional from the point of view of their formal features, although she fully utilizes the achievements of psychological realism. In the field of the novel the situation is quite similar: Dabrowska comes up with a work which follows the best tradition of the realist novel, and that tradition in Poland was quite impressive both in scope and in depth.

II *The Growth of* Nights and Days

As elsewhere, the novel in Poland developed as a distinct literary genre in the eighteenth century. Didactic moralistic prose on the one hand and adventure stories of the *Gesta Romanorum* type on the other, can still be seen in such Polish novels as *The Adventures of Mikolaj Doswiadczynski* (*Mikolaja Doswiadczynskiego przypadki*) by Ignacy Krasicki (1776), *Jan from Tenczyn* (*Jan z Tenczyna*) by Julian Ursyn Niemcewicz (1825), or *A Manuscript Found in Saragossa* by Jan Potocki (published orginally in French, *Manuscript trouvé a Saragosse,* St. Petersburg, 1805; the Polish translation, *Rekopis znaleziony w Saragossie,* was first published in Leipzig in 1847).

Formally, from the point of view of a distinct pattern, develop-

[39]

ment of characters, interplay of themes, etc., all such works were still on a quite basic level. But they did bring literature a little closer to contemporary problems and ideas. The real development of the novel form in Poland, as elsewhere, came during the period of Realism. J. I. Kraszewski was in many respects a precursor of this form in Polish literature, but the real masters were the three great prosaists—Eliza Orzeszkowa, Boleslaw Prus, and Henryk Sienkiewicz. The latter can be especially regarded as a creator of the modern Polish novel. He gave the model of narrative prose which was later followed by all Polish writers, he perfected the basic patterns of plot in both historical fiction and in the contemprary novel, and he even reached into the sphere of psychological realism. Orzeszkowa and Prus, on the other hand, put the Polish novel on the firm ground of vital social problems of both local and universal character (the problem of social and racial equality in Orzeszkowa's peasant and Jewish novels and the problem of human progress versus conservatism in Prus's *Pharao*).

One of the most important postulates of the poetics of Realism was that the characters in fiction should be firmly rooted in real life, that their daily work, earnings, needs and pleasures should be credible, if not authentic. The discovery that even the most angelic heroine must have at least two meals per day, to say nothing of certain other physiological needs, and that even the most romantic hero still has to earn—or steal—his clothes and his daily bread, if he is to go on with his elevated soliloquies, came as a shock to many a writer and reader, but it was soon accepted as a common truth. By concentrating on these perhaps trivial but nevertheless "real" problems of individual and collective life, by making certain social and economic issues the actual theme of literary works, the writers had to arrive at a new concept of such a genre as the novel, a concept according to which the continuity of the inner life of an individual was no longer an absolute center of interest, but had to be correlated with the wider social, political, and economic context. "To understand life and the development of a given artistic form"—writes the Polish critic, S. Brzozowski[4] —"means to understand its relationship to the problems of contemporary life." This is a good example of the extreme consequences drawn from the experience of Realism. In literary practice it meant more and more stress on a strictly materialistic, biological, and sociological concept of individual and collective problems, a concept which received its ultimate exposure in exaggerated naturalism.

The unavoidable reaction came in the form of modernism, which had to wrestle with the "demon" of evolutionism and dialectic materialism, and reinstitute some of the romantic dreams of the power of the individual human spirit, and also the sense of the individual autonomous life of artistic creations. At its best the modernistic novel established a better balance between social issues taken from the point of view of historical materialism and evolutionism, the importance of individual emotional and spiritual qualities, often taken from the revolutionary rather than the evolutionary point of view, and, finally, more free experimentation in artistic forms. In Poland the novels of Stefan Zeromski on the one hand, and the activity of S. Przybyszewski on the other can be quoted as examples of this modernistic struggle against realist conventions. Precursory experiments by Karol Irzykowski and S. I. Witkiewicz have already been mentioned.

Against the background of this tradition in novel writing, Maria Dabrowska's novel does not provide any formal or ideological surprises. But the artistic fulfillment, and the note of deeply human concern and integrity in facing the most vital problems of human life in the past and in the present, combine in an admirable way the main achievements of both realist and modern writing. Interest in individual destinies, fine psychological analyses, the concept of style, all these things bear witness to the author's relationship to her time. At the same time, however, there is nothing loose, accidental, or strictly experimental in her novel, and the individual problems of her heroes are not hanging in the air of social indifference; the fate of each person in the novel is a symbol of the fate of the collective, and the world-outlook of each of the main protagonists is a reflection of the important issues of the collective life. No wonder that the appearance of the novel became the greatest literary event of the decade in Poland. When, one by one, the six volumes of this large novel came out in the short period of time—1932–1934—they were greeted by the almost unanimous enthusiasm of both critics and readers.

The cycle consists of four main parts, the third and fourth of which consist of two volumes each. This tetralogical structure has its internal logic; on the one hand, there is the natural—the biological, as it were—rhythm in the eternal cycles of human life, rotating as the seasons rotate in nature, and on the other hand there are both the ideological and the strictly artistic rhythms dictating this composition. Thus the first volume presents the bringing together of the main heroes of the novel, Bogumil Niechcic and Barbara Ostrzenska, their backgrounds, social positions, marriage. The volume, appropriately titled *Bogumil and Barbara,* appeared in 1932, although, according to the author, the basic idea of a novel devoted to the life of the generation which lived at the turn of the century goes back to the very start of her creative work, and even the names of the main protagonists were clear in her mind at that time. In her article, "How *Nights and Days* was created," published in *Kultura,* No. 7, 1932, Dabrowska gives the following ideological commentary on the genesis of the novel:

> Simultaneously, quite clearly the idea shaped out in my mind of a work depicting people who, at the turn of the century, lived in an isolated countryside where, far away from all the world issues which overshadow the clear lines of the picture, the transformation of one concrete type of life into a different one was to take place.[5]

As we will see, this goal remained one of the chief problems in the eventually completed work.

The actual story of the Niechcic family begins with Bogumil's meeting Barbara and falling in love with this young girl who does not know what she wants, having just been abandoned by the man of her choice. Bogumil is much older and not rich, but he is handsome, energetic, and has a romantic past: participation in the Polish uprising against Russia in 1863 as a boy of fifteen, imprisonment, and adventures abroad. Barbara accepts his abrupt proposal, and after a quick wedding the young couple settles down on the estate which Bogumil manages for a landowner, since his own family estates had been confiscated by the Russians after the uprising. It is now the year 1884 and provincial life in Russian occupied Poland is very uneventful. Bogumil has his work and his love for Barbara; she has neither, not being able to find any meaningful goal in her life with Bogumil. But life goes on; children are born, one of them dies, and Bogumil's work brings results, for he decides to take a bigger estate. The first fourteen or fifteen years of this chronicle of Bogumil's and Barbara's life fill the first volume of the novel. It may seem that nothing much happens in this life, and yet every day of this somewhat strange relationship between the two so different characters is filled with things that are important to them individually and symptomatic for their whole generation.

In the following parts of *Nights and Days* Dabrowska further develops the motifs characteristic of each of the main figures in the work. Part Two, *Eternal Worry* (*Wieczne zmartwienie*), published in the same year, 1932, has Barbara with her constant worry and lack of self-assurance as its main subject matter. In this volume, in the course of just about two years, the fortunes of the Niechcic family improve considerably, Bogumil is successful and satisfied in his work, the three children, Agnieszka, Tomasz, and Emilia grow up normally and happily though not without some troubles, especially in the case of the boy. After the usual and sometimes quite unusual experiences with private teachers, Agnieszka goes to school. Barbara is always worried, dissatisfied with herself and with others, and never completely responsive to Bogumil's love, though he tries hard to make her happy and to free her from her "eternal worry." *Love* (*Milosc*) is the prime motive in his life and that is the title of Part Three of the novel, which appeared in two volumes in 1933. In this part the horizon widens and events of social and political significance enter the quiet provincial life of the Niechcic family: the mobilization of the Russian army for the war against Japan in 1904, unrest in Polish villages in connection with the Revolution of 1905, a workers' demonstration in the city of Kaliniec, and a Polish school strike as witnessed by Agnieszka. But the basic pattern of life in the countryside does not change. Only Agnieszka, who goes abroad to study like the author herself, represents a completely different ideology. This whirlwind of ideas, programs, dreams, in the midst of which crystallize the characters and the ideological beliefs of the young generation, is described in Part Four of *Nights and Days*, which, entitled *Wind in the Eyes* (*Wiatr w oczy*), appeared in 1934, also in two volumes. The main

issues are presented here through the eyes of Agnieszka, who os-
cilates between her father's ideals and the more radical ideology
of her student friends and her husband, Marcin Sniadowski.

In this ideological configuration of the cycle, certain differences
can be seen between Dabrowska's work and those works of world
literature which quite naturally come to mind in looking for possible literary analogies. These works are, of course, Thomas Mann's
story of the decline of the Buddenbrook family (*Buddenbrooks*)
and *The Forsythe Saga* by John Galsworthy. Perhaps also *The
Artamonov Business* by Maxim Gorky can be mentioned here.
Dabrowska, incidentally, has stated that she did not know these
works at that time. In speaking of the existence of many fine examples of this literary form—the family novel—she acknowledges
only her acquaintance with *Kristin Lavransdatter* by Sigrid Undset, making additional reference to *The Hut on the Outskirts of
the Village* by J. I. Kraszewski.[6]

III *Ideological Premises*

As for the ideological content of her work, Dabrowska gave the
following auto-analysis in an interview published in *Kultura* some
time before the appearance of the first volume of the novel:

> The story of Barbara and Bogumil is an attempt at depicting the
> spiritual confusion of that group of the elite of our society—mainly the
> landowning group—which comes from the old landed gentry and
> which is presently losing its social status. Deprived or self-deprived of
> its properties, it loses those forms of religion and morality which previ-
> ously governed its life, and by the natural course of things it tries to
> create a new morality and a new practical philosophy, independent of
> its status and class-affiliation.[7]

This passage was taken up by Henryk Markiewicz, one of the
few consistent and scholarly authoritative Marxist critics in Poland, in his interesting and profound paper, "*Nights and Days*
and the Polish Novelistic Tradition," read at the Commemorative
Session of the Polish Academy of Sciences held in Dabrowska's
honor in May, 1962, and subsequently published in the volume,
Fifty Years of the Creative Work of Maria Dabrowska.[8]

In this article, as in his earlier essay on "Typicality in Polish
literature," [9] Markiewicz puts special emphasis on the problem in

Dabrowska's novel of seeking and formulating new ideological values, on the idea of "man's emancipation from the need to own and accumulate private property." It is in this feature that Markiewicz sees the main difference between Dabrowska's work and the European and Polish novels which also depict the decline of a family or the development of a revolutionary. However, in the light of what Dabrowska said in the above quoted interview, and in the light of the work itself, this is only partly true. Citing Thomas Mann's "bourgeois epos," as an example, we can, with some oversimplification, reduce the main issue there to the problem of the gradual decline of the Buddenbrook family resulting from the betrayal of the tradition of established business principles and *sui generis* morality which were the foundation of the family's wealth and importance.

While it is true that, in comparison, Dabrowska's work is based on the principle of dynamic optimism, of faith in new programs and new values even if they negate and partly destroy the established tradition, in Galsworthy's "saga" we have a not altogether dissimilar situation. Here, too, we have the attachment to tradition and the gradual decline of the importance of the family, a decline connected with the young generation no longer having the same attitude toward private property and social status. But in the position of the author we can discern some of the elements that can be found in Dabrowska: there is in Galsworthy some of the same "epic calmness" in the presentation of this course of life, and there is the same sympathetic attitude toward the natural opposition of the young generation.

Indeed, the whole problem of Dabrowska's position is not as clear as it may seem from Markiewicz's interpretation. The ideals of Bogumil Niechcic are not so radically different from the ideals of his ancestors. To be sure, his social position is different, he is no longer a rich landowner; but in his work as an administrator and subsequently as a lease-holder, and finally as an owner, he is not entirely free from dreams of accumulating material wealth and acquiring his own estate. Though it would not be an inherited estate, and though it would be only a measly two *wloki* (33 acres), nevertheless it is still a dream based on the "old" capitalistic principle. Only toward the end, shortly before Bogumil's death, does there come a moment of sublimation of this dream.

Sublimation seems the best term for the phenomenon, since it is not a radical change of character, not a real "transformation"; it is only a moment of a better realization of certain truths which have not been quite clear to the hero, and which, as with Dionysius in *People from Yonder,* are suddenly revealed to him in their full significance:

After all, how did he differ from all these people? He liked to eat and drink well, as did they, he liked to farm, hardly noticing anything beyond the limits of the estate, and in moments of leisure he liked to enjoy life and nature. Country life makes one inclined to enjoy the sky and the landscape after work, to live on the harvest without desiring anything else. He now owned an estate as others did; well, somewhat smaller, but still . . . his family tradition and his past in Jarosty would make up for what may be lacking in the number of acres.

He recalled how, years ago, having a good time with some dinner guests, he himself maintained that when a man did his job with planting and harvest, and when his conscience is clear, then what more does he need? It seemed to him then that this was the foundation of the world. Yes, today, too, he could repeat it, and yet he felt that in this simple concept of life he saw something more than the people with whom he dined. Seemingly he was identical with them, and yet he was different. Yes, Barb was right. Circumstances could have returned him to his place among the landowners, but one really never returns where one once had left. Has something shifted in him in a different direction? Perhaps only his children will know what. He knew that earthly goods, even the thought of gaining them and keeping and enjoying them, was no longer his main preoccupation day and night as it used to be.

But neither did he clearly see the ultimate goal, the reason for which he did all this. All his life he occupied a middle position from which, as on a hike, one can no longer see the place of departure, and, at the same time, one cannot see the place where one is going. Barbara was tortured by this, but he could take it, since he, with both his hands and eyes, was submerged in work as if it were the salvation. And to be such a wanderer, not attached to anything stable, relying exclusively on productive work, isn't that the real position of a man? On work, and perhaps on . . .[10]

It is quite characteristic of Dabrowska's ideological attitude that when it comes to formulating certain cardinal truths about man's position in the world, the thinking of an educated representative of the higher class does not basically differ from the thinking of a simple uneducated farmhand. For Bogumil Niechcic it is just as hard to realize the full meaning of his life as it is for Dionysius in *People from Yonder*. For him, too, the truth comes as a rare moment of "dazzlement," a moment which he would hardly be able to re-create again:

> Something was rising within him and growing into a song which was about to articulate into melody and words. He labored hard at getting it out, till it finally developed into a thought, clear as crystal:
> "At the same plough you see God or just a clod of earth. Looking at the same tree you see the miracle of creation or just shadow, leaves, fruit, or building material . . ."
> This thought was still rising upward, and a still more perfect formulation of the secret of life and of the world was about to reveal itself—when suddenly it broke apart and vanished.
> It happened so suddenly that after just a short while Bogumil hardly knew what he was thinking. . ." [11]

As we can see, here, as in *People from Yonder*, the emphasis is rather on the moral-spiritual issue than on the strictly social problem of to-have-or-not-to-have. Dabrowska's thoughts circle around the wider, universal problem of human happiness as correlated to man's capacity for self-denial and sacrifice. And what is important is the fact that in this respect her heroes are, above all, human beings, regardless of their social position. Just as Bogumil does in the above quoted passage, so on many other occasions, other representatives of the educated class express views which are identical to the views of illiterate peasants in her stories. When the highly sophisticated engineer Ceglarski philosophises in *Nights and Days*, he occasionally repeats almost literally some of the thoughts of the uneducated Dionysius from *People from Yonder*. His paradox, namely that in order "to find oneself one has to forget oneself," is a direct echo of Dionysius' paradox that "when one loses all hope, then only can one see that he has not lost anything."

In an interview granted the author of this book in May, 1964, the seventy-five year old writer glanced back once more at her novel—which meanwhile had had sixteen editions, and which is one of the most admired works in Polish literature—and elaborated on some of the things she had said before. She admitted that many of the things said by various critics are right, but she insisted that, above all, it is the interest and love for human life, the psychological rather than ideological insights that are the substance of her work.

Almost simultaneously with her earlier quoted self-analysis in *Kultura*, Dabrowska stated that she consciously avoided creating a novel with a message. Her rationale from this point of view is quite simple and quite convincing:

Before *Nights and Days* appeared, several people asked me whether my novel had a guiding thought—and what it may be. And this is a timely question. The world is so tired of the successes of literary technique that it longs to go back to the good old novel with a message. But this is the desire to go from one extreme to another, and I must say that I tried to resist such temptation. In *Nights and Days* there is actually no guiding thought in the strict intellectual meaning of this word. At the same time I am convinced that if I myself possess—consciously or unconsciously—a guiding thought in life, character, and spiritual attitude toward the world, all this will unavoidably find its artistic reflection in the content of my work . . .[12]

Of course, the main personages in her novel, Bogumil Niechcic and Barbara, his wife, and their daughter Agnieszka, are representatives of a larger group. Of course they may be called "typical" both as representatives of these groups and also as representatives of a certain kind of character. But they are, above all, individual human characters, created by the artistic power of the writer, each one of them living in the particular reality not imitated but evoked by the artist as something independent and unique, though, at the same time, highly real. Human heart, human soul as something sacred and infinitely valuable by itself, but at the same time as something that can hardly exist for itself, without the element of love and of compassion for other human beings, this is, perhaps, the most important factor in Dabrowska's work. It crystallized very early in her life and it remained with her as possibly the only true "guiding thought."

Perhaps the best illustration of this is the fine portrait of Agnieszka Niechcic, the young daughter of Bogumil and Barbara. In the process of changes depicted in *Nights and Days*, Agnieszka represents the generation which already is free from the tradition of possessing land as the symbol of social status; she possesses a new set of values, based entirely on character, profession, ideas, and a somewhat vague program, connected with bettering the political, social, and economic lot of people. Like the author herself, she leaves home to go abroad for study, and like the author herself, she studies natural sciences in Switzerland. Like the author herself, she finds a man who is an active political agent with radical socialist affiliations. But this, of course, does not mean that Agnieszka is the author's only *porte parole*. Dabrowska herself stated emphatically that if any of the personages expresses her own views, then it is above all Bogumil. Actually, all three of the main personages can be said to express some of the author's ideas. Only when taken together and supplemented by many other figures in the novel can they give a sum of things that are close to the author's heart. This polyphonic ideological concept is in agreement with the practice of realism.

Agnieszka, nevertheless, often seems to express better than any other person in the novel some of the thoughts which were mentioned above as the most essential in Dabrowska's concept of human life and of the place of an individual in society. In her conversations with Boleslaw Orlowicz, Agnieszka sometimes formulates her most intimate thoughts on this point:

You know, I often think that only something very simple can lead us—in the meaning of a guiding star. . . . Let us call it God, love, the sacredness of another human being, faithfulness to oneself or rather to something that is in us that is bigger than we are. Generalities, you will think? No. These are fundamental truths of life. There are such truths. And they decide ultimately about war and peace. I know, she added, that it is difficult to recognize something as a necessity and yet stop short of making a fetish out of it.[13]

In Agnieszka's idealistic reasoning, it is easy to observe certain analogies—both ideological and stylistic—to Stefan Zeromski's works. The conversations between Agnieszka and Orlowicz sometimes seem almost a direct echo of certain parts of Zeromski's *Before the Spring* (*Przedwiosnie*). In both cases one can speak of a certain amount of naïve sentimentalism, and in both cases one can discern certain remnants of Romanticism in its typically Polish version. In Agnieszka's attitude toward religion there is also some analogy to Zeromski, or, perhaps, one should rather say that her attitude is typical of a large group of the Polish intelligentia. This attitude can be best seen in Agnieszka's conversation with the parish priest in Part IV. It demonstrates a mixture of abstract beliefs in religious ideals and scepticism toward their more practical aspects, especially toward the narrow-mindedness of some representatives of the clergy and the rigid church organization. Agnieszka, like some of Zeromski's heroes, blames the church for being more concerned with discipline and propaganda than with real human needs and ideals. It must be added that in *Nights and Days* the whole problem is by no means one-sidedly presented; the priest with whom Agnieszka hesitantly enters into a discussion of her thoughts and doubts is depicted as a simple but highly human, tolerant, and idealistic clergyman. His understanding attitude toward Agnieszka's doubts is another example of Dabrowska's ability to avoid oversimplification in her fictional presentation of serious problems.

In this respect, of course, H. Markiewicz's remarks about the "typical" elements in Dabrowska's work are partly justified. Her heroes, their problems and their reasoning, are sufficiently authentic from the point of view of problems and mentalities typical of a large group of the Polish intelligentsia; and Dabrowska consciously strove to recreate some of the problems and some of the mentalities that were typical of the older and the younger generations in Poland at the turn of the century. She is fully aware of the fact that these processes are closely related to the social and economic changes, and she does not hesitate to tackle these problems through the reactions of various people in her novel. Primarily, however, she is interested in the psychological aspects of these reactions, in the processes of life as they are reflected in the individual characters and in their inter-relations.

The most important question for me [said Dabrowska in her statement in *Wiadomosci Literackie* after the publication of the first volume of *Nights and Days*] was the problem as to how this phase of transition from one world to another is reflected in the two so different attitudes toward life as represented by Bogumil and Barbara; the essential feature in Barbara being the struggle against herself and against the world, struggle intensified by fear and by an excess of imagination, while in Bogumil it is courage, some kind of inherent ability to perform creative work in the spot chosen by fate, and it is peace, love, community with life and a certain spiritual passivity.[14]

A few years later, when the whole cycle was completed, Dabroska again repeated her preoccupation with this problem of the relationship between the two diametrically different characters. In her article, "A Few Thoughts on *Nights and Days*," ("Kilka mysli o Nocach i Dniach"), published in *Atheneum*, No. 4-5, 1938, Dabrowska lists this theme as the first one of the many motifs developed in her work. She describes it as "the theme of two psychological formations, two kinds of people, two spiritual attitudes toward reality; the one, in harmony with life, active, open toward the world; the other, in disagreement with life, full of anxiety and suspicions, closed toward life." [15] Furthermore, Dabrowska points out, this opposition of characters can be extended as a motif which can be seen in almost all of the secondary figures in the work, without the author's direct approval or disapproval of the one or the other of these types. This attitude of watching and examining the manifestations of the basic features in human character "with love and compassion," yet sufficiently objectively not to condemn or glorify, bears witness to the author's epic talent.

What furthermore interested the writer—and what partly escaped the attention of the critics—was the intricate problem of the mutual relationship of these two people: Bogumil's steady though perhaps somewhat "unromantic" love for Barbara for a long time remains unrequited. And yet, Barbara gradually learns to rely on it completely and eventually finds herself in a position in which she can hardly exist without it. The image of her first—real or imaginary—love for another man fades from her feelings.

Thus, in all the contrasts there is also analogy between these two characters. For example, Bogumil's thoughts about the sense of life find an echo in Barbara when, having lost both Bogumil and material security, she finally finds herself at peace with life. Looking back on her long life with Bogumil, she could say with Kristin Lavransdatter that in spite of everything she really loved this life against which she had revolted in the past:

Having exhausted all the despair that the human heart can endure, these verses led imperceptibly but unfailingly toward joy as night leads toward day.

Perhaps it is possible then that all this must lead to joy, to love of life—whatever life is: a ladder-step of providence or a spark between nothingness and nothingness again, happiness of your home's thresh-hold, triumph of widespread activity, or a road in the darkness of night and in the light of conflagration into the unknown.

Barbara felt strengthened as people are strengthened when they forget themselves in prayer, and she finally began to feel so completely herself and at home, as if this rattling carriage were a haven to which she had been travelling all her life.[16]

Bogumil's character is stronger and less complicated, and so is his love for Barbara. But he is not free from weaknesses, he has his doubts—his "rises and falls." In her striving for a complete and true picture Dabrowska does not shy away from erotic themes. Especially in *People from Yonder*, but also in *Nights and Days*, there are some realistic scenes of sexual passion which some critics found excessive. And, of course, even her most "positive" hero, Bogumil, is not free from sexual temptations (and their fulfill-ment). There is Bogumil's fascination with a young girl, Miss Woynarowska, a fascination which he succeeds in overcoming—in a moving scene in the girl's bedroom—realizing that he would ruin both the girl's life and his own family. Then there is a primitive fulfillment of physical passion with the children's nurse, a simple peasant woman. Nevertheless, these aspects of human life do not overshadow other problems—intellectual, moral, ideological—in Dabrowska's works.[17]

In our interview in Warsaw, Dabrowska made mention of the problem of Barbara's development and Bogumil's "rises and falls," motifs more important than was generally realized. She also stressed on that occasion the problem of her presentation of the social changes in her novel. This is not a single-direction process, as would have been the case in a typically tendentious social novel, but an objectively observed course of currents and cross-currents, a course in which—as in real life—there is an osmosis of social groups, decomposition of some and formation of others, and constant movment in both directions. While some people become detached from the property-owning group and begin forming new ideals, others take up the very desire to possess worldly goods and make that their goal in life. All these currents can be observed at work, making it all the more full and convincing as a realistic novel.

IV *The Simplest Truths*

In trying to assess the ideological content of Dabrowska's work one is often struck by certain analogies, or at least similarities, to the work of Joseph Conrad. It is not so much in the situations in which the author puts her heroes as in their views on life and on human destiny in the world that these similarities can be seen. Sometimes it will be paradox, like Heyst's victory in defeat in Conrad's *Victory* and Barbara's finding peace and safety in losing all material security. More often it will be some very simple and old truth whose novelty lies in the unique set of circumstances which lead to such a re-statement of otherwise known thoughts.

Shortly before she started her work on the novel *Nights and Days*, Dabrowska displayed a deeper interest in Conrad's works which at that time were appearing one by one in Polish translation. Although Dabrowska possessed a good knowledge of English (during the war she translated S. Pepys' *Diary*, published in parts in various periodicals and in book form, *Dziennik, 1–2,* in 1952) there is not much evidence of her interest in Conrad prior to the appearance of the Polish translations. However, her remarks on the translations point to her acquaintance with the originals. In her review of the Polish translation of *Nostromo*, in *Wiadomosci Literackie,* 1929, we can find an excellent example of the kind of ideological, or moral, affinity which was mentioned above. In her reflections on the problem of moral values as opposed to material wealth as presented in Conrad's novel, Dabrowska pointed out some things which she found of special interest and which later found a clear echo in her own work. For example, Dabrowska mentions Conrad's resolution of the conflict over the silver treasure as one of the most significant aspects of *Nostromo*. She echoes Conrad's anti-materialistic formula of the treasure, "the loss of which won't make a single man poorer" by her own slogan: "Let the treasure perish, if it becomes the people's master instead of servant." [18]

It is not surprising to see that in *Nostromo* Dabrowska singles out the following thought expressed by the railroad engineer:

Upon my word, doctor, things seem to be worth nothing by what they are in themselves. I begin to believe that the only solid thing about them is the spiritual value which everyone discovers in his own form of activity.[19]

It is probably not a sheer coincidence that Bogumil Niechcic, who like the engineer in *Nostromo* is a man of action, comes to realize more and more that the real value in a man's life is the quality of his productive work.

Dabrowska ends her review of Conrad's *Nostromo* with some comments which strengthen the impression that even though one can hardly speak of any direct literary influence, nevertheless there is a spiritual kinship between these two writers. After having mentioned some of the ideological aspects in Conrad which she considers particularly important, Dabrowska gives a concluding statement which almost can be regarded as her artistic and ideological credo:

These are simple, almost crude truths, but in all that the human race achieves and loses through science, progress, and organization, it is really nourished by just a few truths and moral principles, principles which it constantly betrays, but for which it longs and to which it always returns.

And the greatest writers are those who are able to evoke out of the chaos of their time one of these age-old principles and show it in a new light for people to believe in it.[20]

Dabrowska has emphatically denied statements made by some critics that her own views are expressed mainly in the ideological portrait of Agnieszka. And yet, one cannot help feeling that somehow in Agnieszka's idealistic enthusiasm there is an important part of the author's dreams, that what Dabrowska as a realistic writer had to give up in the name of epic objectivity, in portraying Bogumil and Barbara, she allowed herself to ascribe to this naïve young girl. Perhaps one can risk the conjecture that the author, while creating the realistic vision of the existing world of the parents, allowed herself to give a more idealized vision of her own youthful dreams in the character of Agnieszka as she herself once was or wanted to be.

There is nothing exceptional about Agnieszka's personality. She is one of the three children of the Niechcic couple and her upbringing follows a perfectly normal course. But of the three children, she is the one that seems to interest the writer most of all, and her course is very similar indeed to that of the writer herself. She goes to school in the nearby city, and her school years are described very vividly and in great detail in regard to her inner life and to her rapidly developing interest in serious questions, her deep concern with the social and moral problems of her life. The period of her studies abroad in Switzerland bears an especially clear imprint of the author's personal experience. Her interests, her journalistic work for the cooperative movement, her contacts with political émigré circles, her involvement with a socialist activist, all this is described with unmistakable autobiographical insight. Agnieszka's journalistic writing ventures alone make her close to the author's heart, and we can see that she even expresses some views on the art of writing which are Dabrowska's.

Agnieszka's main concern in life is the place, destiny, and responsibility of the individual. Somewhat like Pasternak's Doctor Zhivago, she regards life as something wonderful, and she sees the individual's right to it as the most sacred thing on earth. In the pursuit of the right to live one's own life, she wants the individual to be free both from the exploitation of capitalism and the absolute regimentation of life by socialist collective. This maximalistic and idealistic, mainly humanitarian, program which has very little to do with practical politics of the people with whom the young Agnieszka associates, was, of course, an echo of the early idealistic phase of socialism. In terms of political programs it would have to be associated with anarchism in the Christian spirit on the one hand, and with some syndicalist notions on the other; but Dabrowska does not resolve her ideological problems on the level of practical political programs, and thus—not unlike Stefan Zeromski in some of his novels—can allow herself to dream of this kind of moral purification which would enable people to improve their collective social and economic situation without encroaching on the sovereign right of the individual. Not without some justification this concept has been termed a naïve illusion by both Agnieszka's more politically-minded friends in the novel and by some critics in Poland. To the extent that a writer bears responsibility for the views of his heroes, Dabrowska shares the honor of being regarded as an ideological utopianist with such writers as Leo Tolstoy and Stefan Zeromski.

And, as indicated above, there cannot be much doubt that the views of the main characters of *Nights and Days* are indeed, to a high degree, the writer's own. Dabrowska even tried in some instances to translate her artistic vision into the language of practical politics where she directly pointed out the implications of some experiences of her heroes. These attempts, of course, were not very successful. In 1937, when the economic situation in the overpopulated Polish villages was very bad, and political unrest among the peasant masses was growing fast while little was being done about the long-promised land reform, Dabrowska published a political pamphlet, *Crossroads* (*Rozdroze*) in which, as a writer and as a former social worker, she called for more efficient land reform and optimistically but unrealistically tried to convince the Polish landowners that they should be more magnanimous and not obstruct the process. In her laudable attempt to talk sense to both the adherents of more radical social measures and the conservative circles which tried to prevent any changes, Dabrowska found herself in the hopeless situation of an idealist meddler who spoke of "moral transformation," "moral treasures" and so forth where the issue concerned the economic interest of the property owners on the one hand and hungry millions on the other. Like Turgenev in Russia, Dabrowska turned out to be too progressive to please the conservatives and not sufficiently revolutionary to satisfy the radicals. She became involved in lengthy polemics in which she did not seem able to distinguish between the artistic vision of her literary works and the reality of practical politics. Having set out to offend no one, she ended by pleasing none.

Recalling her presentation of the ideological development of Bogumil from *Nights and Days,* Dabrowska calls in her polemic for a "spiritual liberation from the desire to own property" similar to the one her literary hero was able to achieve in a rare moment of self-penetration: "What is needed, is to experience the moment of revelation that nothing earthly, nothing material, can be a dogma or an exclusive goal in life." [21]

Nights and Days

It is mainly in her long conversations with Boleslaw Orlowicz that Agnieszka expresses her ideas, her inner thoughts, her doubts and expectations. The recurring motif in these conversations is her concern with the imponderables of human life, with such things as freedom of conscience and integrity of character. She admits that in order to improve the lot of millions, radical social changes may be needed, but she is frightened at the thought of the possible infringement on individual rights. She would like to see all this happen through the same magic "transformation" of human beings, their instincts, their egoism, their attachment to earthly wealth.

You see—Agnieszka saddened again—you said something about character. And yet it is not character that we propagate. Discipline, obedience . . . I agree with that . . . And you, and Martin . . . And you know why, you know that this won't hurt your goal. But for the millions of people this will just be the line of least resistance, shirking personal responsibility, to build this very character. They will be disciplined for they won't be capable of anything else, of creative transformation of themselves. And that is what people need. Everyone.

And what if this transformation of men is impossible—Orlowicz asked with a hostile whisper—What if you only can mold them, use them for something which only a few see and know? Perhaps sometimes only one single person? [22]

Later Agnieszka returns to this conversation and on that occasion she develops her thoughts into a manifesto of faith in the priority of spiritual values in human life.

You said, "and what if people cannot change?" No, Bolek, in that case the world would be just a cruel joke of a malicious God. Perhaps people are like stars and suns in the universe which rotate within the closed system without any purpose outside of just existing. And yet, what do we know about the changes and processes of improvement that occur in these rotating systems? It is enough to look at the world of vegetation or animals. How many changes man himself has been able to cause. Why then could not he change himself, better himself, prepare for more honorable struggle than mutual killing? Perhaps he does not even have to change, perhaps he only has to discover himself, to reveal the ability to live a full life so that he could see beyond himself, to see other people, society, eternal things. . . .

Oh yes—she recalled after a moment of silence—I used to have different thoughts about it, but now I know. You believe that a man can only be used so that he can serve the purpose of humanity mechanically in the mass. And I want to tell you that the real purpose is only one: man himself, real, live man. He is the source, he is the measure of everything. . . . Not in himself, but because only in a living man, national, social . . . religious phenomena can develop all that reaches higher than a man. Well, even Socialism . . . not in the meaning of a political party or some kind of didactics, but in a deeper, spiritual meaning. Isn't it so that his only true revolution was when he said: not business, not money, profit, machine . . . in other words, not all the material products, but MAN, PEOPLE should govern life; people, living people, she repeated almost like a maniac.[23]

To be a man, to be human, to respect other human beings, to be faithful to one's human destiny, one's work, one's place in the world—all this belongs to the sphere of the "simple, almost crude truths" which Dabrowska sees in life and which she again and again reveals to her readers in various situations, stated and re-stated by various people as something familiar, almost trite but nonetheless important. And the writer's instinct proved right, the instinct which let her sense that in the midst of expressionistic experiments in prose and avant-garde innovations in poetry, people could receive these simple ideas as something important and worth admiration. This was mainly because each of the characters in Dabrowska *was* a fully developed, live character, a human being who was at the same time universal and unique. This, of course, was the secret of the writer's artistic talent.

But it must be stressed, once more, that only taken as a whole—as the sum of the views of all the main and some of the secondary characters, the sum of their actions and of the author's direct or indirect comments—only all these things together can be regarded as the novel's ideological "message." It is not a social message, a formula for re-shaping the world, nor even for improving this or that aspect of collective life. Dabrowska's message, if we insist on searching for it, is simply that each human life is something valuable, something fascinating, something which is given to men as a wonderful, sacred gift. It is their privilege and their duty to pursue it to the best of their moral, intellectual, and physical abilities. The writer's task is simply to portray it with interest and understanding, to live it with the people in his work as fully and faithfully as his vision of life permits.

As for me [Dabrowska said in the interview in *Wiadomosci Literackie* concerning *Nights and Days*] I simply wanted to express in this novel my love for the unceasingly flowing and passing life, love, which exists without regard to whether this life is just a tiny spark in the midst of chaos and darkness or a stage on the road toward great and fateful goals.[24]

CHAPTER 3

Nights and Days—*Problems of Style*

"Quand on voit le style naturel, on est tout étonné: car on s'attendait de voir un auteur, et on trouve un homme."

Pascal

I *Modernized Realism*

WHEN *Nights and Days* appeared, literary critics explained the enthusiastic reception of this novel as largely due to the fact that readers in Poland were tired of the forced style of frequently amorphous expressionist works without easily perceivable substance, and thus were happy to receive a well-built traditional novel where, without any special effort, they found real characters, real life events composed in a well-proportioned unit with the narrative stream following the principles of logic, probability, and chronology. All this is partly—but only partly—true.

Nights and Days starts as a typical traditional novel of the 19th century. It looks as if the author were going to take the full course of novel exposition, introducing the reader to the history and prehistory of the main characters so as to have the reader fully prepared for the events that constitute the theme of the work. However, this first impression of orderly chronological progress is somewhat deceptive. Contrary to what most critics said about the good old solid technique of *Nights and Days*, some signs of more modern devices are discernible almost from the start.

The best illustration of this technique is the treatment of the hero, Bogumil Niechcic. After some rather sketchy remarks about his background and youth, the author leaves out a somewhat mysterious "heroic" period of his life, so important to the formation of his character, namely his participation as a sixteen-year-old boy in the Polish uprising aginst the Russians in 1863 and his life in exile after the defeat. The novel actually begins at the moment when the hero as a forty-five-year-old man falls in love with the young

Barbara. Only retrospectively, at various points in the work, does the author reveal certain aspects of this period of Bogumil's life. This happens when it becomes necessary for a better psychological motivation of certain situations and certain decisions on the part of Bogumil.

There can be no doubt that this mode of narration is not a coincidence, but a conscious technique on Dabrowska's part. The device of selection, of eliminating certain stages of development from their chronological place as if hiding them from the reader, is a well-known technique, which often serves the purpose of creating a mysterious aura and intensifying the dramatic quality of situations in which a certain character is brought into contact with other people, or with fate, or with some problems and conflicts within.

The whole problem in the case of *Nights and Days* is complicated by the fact that the novel was not written in a normal order. From Dabrowska's account of "How *Nights and Days* was Created" [1] we learn that the first to be written was Volume Two. Its first version, written in 1927–28, was orginally published in installments in the weekly *Kobieta wspolczesna* (*The Modern Woman*); the second version, written soon thereafter and published in the daily *Gazeta Zachodnia* (*Western Gazette*) had an introductory chapter on the history of the families of Bogumil and Barbara. This chapter, according to the author's account, was later expanded into a full volume (Volume One), entitled *Bogumil and Barbara*, while the rest of this version became Volume Two, *Eternal Worry*, soon followed by Volume Three, *Love*, and Volume Four, *Wind in the Eyes*.

Dabrowska's account of this creative process poses an interesting problem so far as the structure of the novel is concerned. Apparently the writer started the work somewhat in the short-story fashion, placing her hero at a certain point, in the midst of the stream of his life, without the traditional preamble which would enable the reader to follow the formation of his character and the background of his ideological profile. It may be said that the conventions of the novelistic technique had forced themselves upon the writer as her work started growing into something of larger proportion than she originally planned—into a fully developed epic novel.

Still, in its final shape the work must be regarded as a closed novelistic structure, and as such it presents the problem of a compromise between the traditional concept of a chronologically composed work and a more modern concept of arranging events in a different order, allowing for a free movement back and forth in time.

Of course, it is impossible definitely to determine to what extent this technique is a consciously conceived and consistently pursued method and to what extent it may be a spontaneous process of evoking life from recollections and observations as they come out of memory when thinking back, and thus re-creating a given vision of reality. Dabrowska made some interesting comments on the problem of personal recollections of a writer in his literary work. She confirms the importance of such recollections in the work of an artist, but she points out that the problem is much more complicated than it appeared to some critics who assumed that, for example, the volume *People from Yonder* was nothing but a collection of memories from Dabrowska's observations of country life as she remembered it from her childhood. Dabrowska analyzes the problem of depicting the reality in her volume as "transposing into the past the reality of the present (amalgamated, of course, by way of a mysterious process, with direct recollections)." [2]

Here, again, a certain analogy with the work of Joseph Conrad must be pointed out. In Conrad's case, we observe a similar phenomenon of oscillating between the traditional chronological method of re-constructing a given course of events and the more modern device (later so often used in movie technique) of reversing this course, of moving back from a certain point in order to illuminate this or that element from the past, and in this way to motivate or intensify the dramatic situations and the decisions of his heroes. Both Conrad and Dabrowska display a high degree of ability to combine in their creative work the process of spontaneous recollections with a carefully planned, strictly artistic vision in which these recollections in spite of their spontaneity are skillfully arranged so as to increase the suspense by surrounding the heroes and their final fate with a certain mysterious aura. This procedure results in an impression of intensified realism, since, after all, life is seldom as orderly as in "well-composed" novels where the author carefully arranges the events so there are no inconsistencies.

Conrad's well-known formula of complete spontaneity in his literary work is, of course, a myth. Although Conrad complained, for example, that his "Outpost of Progress" was a failure because he tried to write it from beginning to end according to a rigid plan,[3] in actual fact Conrad's deeply reflective and disciplined nature as a writer points to the fact that the spontaneity of what he calls "re-creating recollections as they come" was rarely the actual procedure in his writing process. Indeed, it often appears to be exactly the opposite. A more careful analysis of his works frequently leads to the conclusion that the impression of spontaneity is achieved by way of carefully planned and distributed devices. One of these devices is closely associated with the a-chronological presentation of events. It is a device of surrounding the hero with an aura of secrecy and of keeping the reader in suspense, unveiling certain details only by an elaborate step by step process of direct and indirect confrontation of his various aspects so that not until the end is it possible for the reader to perceive the full significance of all these elements—all the allusions, remarks, and actions of the main hero and of the other characters. Of course this method can easily be overdone and Conrad did not escape some criticism on this point. Whereas Mary Burchard Orvis considers this technique of "implying character" as superior, another critic, Walter T. Wright, speaks here of a "weakness of elaboration." [4]

To summarize the above remarks, there is no doubt that what Conrad calls a spontaneous, planless process, is actually in most cases an artful contruction planned and executed very carefully and with the highest degree of precision down to the smallest detail. And there is little doubt that in the case of Maria Dabrowska, the element of purposefulness in artistic proportions of the entire construction is equally important. The impression of spontaneity thus achieved is a matter of individual talent in each case; the total effect of artistic devices creates an impression of a completely natural style because the author in each case has been able to harmonize the formal stylistic means for depicting and arranging events with his ultimate vision of the universal truth of the fulfillment of human destiny.

In contrast to Conrad, Maria Dabrowska has even openly acknowledged her awareness of the function of the "technique of mystery" in her literary works. In her "A Few Thoughts on *Nights and Days*" published in *Atheneum* in 1938, Dabrowska makes the following comment in defense of leaving out certain elements in the process of creating her literary characters. Though made specifically on this particular point, Dabrowska's remarks bear indirectly on her entire method of composition:

If some of my characters are surrounded with an aura of secrecy, or if they got submerged in the stream of events as if silenced or insufficiently explained, I think I endowed them with just as much of this element of secrecy as was needed in order to attain a stronger impression of truth and to achieve a better perspective of the whole vision. Literary figures cannot be seen on one plane, they must appear in close-ups and shown at a distance, and sometimes, shown at a distance they may become hazy and perhaps vanish entirely. In the composition of a work of art, darkness, shadows, haziness are equally legitimate as bright colors and full lights. And in a novel, involving several levels and dimensions, only the participation of all these means gives a whole which breathes with truth and plasticity and which is artistically complete.[5]

It can be seen from these remarks that for Dabrowska this whole question is an integral part of her concept of realism, of her idea of a writer's duty to strive for the fullest and most truthful vision of life possible. This, according to the critic Karol W. Zawodzinski, is one of the real reasons for the tremendous response her work has had. Zawodzinski sees in Dabrowska's artistic victory all the signs of a new literary epoch, which he terms as a period of "modernized realism."

It should again be emphasized that all the remarks in this study on certain similarities in the artistic techniques of Joseph Conrad and Maria Dabrowska are in no way intended to imply a literary influence. It is simply a matter of certain analogies in the philosophy of life and philosophy of writing that can be discerned in these two otherwise so totally different writers. While it may help the English-speaking reader to better appreciate certain aspects of Dabrowska's work if he realizes some of the similarities to an English writer, it should be clear that Dabrowska is an accomplished artist in her own right, without need of a crutch to lean on. This goes for both the ideological and the formal aspect of her work.

II *The Making of Characters*

The novel *Nights and Days* is an artistic organism which lives its own individual life as a complete and independent work, carefully planned, fully developed, finished up to the most minute detail and, at the same time, fresh in its perfect simplicity and clarity of style, development of characters, themes, and ideas.

There are hardly any paper-figures in this novel, figures needed only as the author's mouthpieces to preach her ideas; all its people are natural and alive. Those among them who are closest to the author's heart—Bogumil, Barbara, Agnieszka, Ceglarski—are not idealized; indeed all of them possess enough of both positive features and weaknesses to be convincing in their reality. Those (perhaps too few) figures who are more negatively treated by the author—Anselm, Katelba, Daleniecki—are not onesidedly painted, and this again makes them more real. The best example of Dabrowska's sense of proportion in the distribution of lights and shadows in sketching her characters is the treatment of the three children of Bogumil and Barbara, Agnieszka, the most "positive" type, Thomas who is almost the opposite, negative, egoistic character and Emily, neutral, somewhat pale, but sufficiently human in her moral passivity.

Secondary figures, too, are needed not only for background. Each of the almost countless gallery of country and city people, landowners, ex-landowners, businessmen, professional people, politicians, peasants, hired hands, are depicted with enough realism, with ample interest in each of them as individuals. There are traces of the author's careful chiseling of details in the characterization of some of these figures, so that by means of a few stylistic changes they appear in a different light; the function of the same details may change completely and even turn in the opposite direction. The Polish critic, Ewa Korzeniewska, has pointed out such instances in her essay on Dabrowska.[6] She has done this by comparing examples from the first, artistically and ideologically not quite thought-through version, originally published in the popular magazine *Modern Woman,* with the final version, when the same material had been incorporated as Volume Two of the tetralogy.

One of the most striking examples of such revision is a passage in which Barbara and Bogumil make some observations about the old Jewish woman, Arkuszowa. We see how the same details, with slight changes in the light of the reflections they evoke, acquire a completely different function in the work.

In the earlier version Bogumil and Barbara react with indifference and even contempt to the appearance of the old woman, to her "badly fitted wig, her pale eyes, her mouth, soft and wrinkled as a tobacco pouch."

When they left her, they said, condemning Jews as a whole: "All the time they go around and scent business."

The same details, very slightly re-touched ("Hemp wig; pale-blue and bloodshot eyes") in the final version of Volume Two provoke completely different reflections on the part of Barbara:

How worn out and miserable she is, she thought. And moved by compassion, she started talking with her about the new worries connected with bringing up children.[7]

These and other similar changes witness both to the writer's deepening concern with the consistency of the ideological profile of her heroine and to her deepening understanding of the secrets of realism as the art of revealing in a uniform vision not only the outer details of human life, but also their emotional and moral significance.

Of course, it is true that so far as the above scene is concerned, the change is mainly ideological. Against the background of growing anti-Semitism this shift of emphasis stresses the author's greater ideological maturity and her growing concern for the need of a real community between people from various groups. This was a sign of the moral integrity which Dabrowska demonstrated on many occasions, publicly protesting against such acts of disregard for law as the imprisonment by the Pilsudski government of the leaders of the political opposition, the sabotaging of the land reform, the "disgrace" of anti-Semitic excesses, and the official permission of "ghetto" rules in accomodating students at Polish universities.

As was pointed out, Dabrowska's method of portraying people and events is highly realistic. She does it, in most cases, not by way of sharp climactic clashes of characters or an artificially staggered maze of situations leading to a tragedy, but rather in a broad perspective of the normal stream of everyday life flowing freely, and often capriciously, in her work, as it does in the life of every one of us. The ability to fuse together the most common, typical, everyday elements with some unique human reactions to these ordinary situations seems to be the secret of any true work of art. This is exactly what is the main feature of realism. It has been said that Dabrowska's novel, *Nights and Days,* is one of the fullest and most vivid presentations of a whole epoch. We recognize without any difficulty the historical period, the national and social features of the time, the whole style of life visible in the people's manners, their speech, their views on moral, social, and political problems; we recognize certain slogans, phrases, words as characteristic of certain circles and situations; we even know what books are being read, what shows are being played, what painters are popular, and so forth. At the same time, we are constantly aware of the fact that all these familiar things do not deprive the people depicted in the novel of their specific features, features which make them individual human beings, living their own individual lives.

III *The Invisible Style*

It has been said that the re-creation of a wide stream of everyday life is the substance of any true epic work. Julian Przybos recalled, in his tribute to Maria Dabrowska at the celebration of her fifty years of creative work, how the concept of epos has changed in more recent times from the idea of a work depicting unusual heroic deeds to the conviction that it is ordinary everyday life that constitutes its substance:

The critics are unanimous—said Przybos—in their praises of Maria Dabrowska as an epic writer; both in her *People from Yonder* and in *Nights and Days* they see the symptoms of epic style. What is the essence of an epos? Since the time of the Alexandrine commentators whole libraries have been written on this subject. During the last two centuries nearly all aesthetic features attributed to what used to be termed "heroic song" have been turned inside out, and today we are inclined to think that not the extraordinary but, on the contrary, the ordinary everyday elements are the natural epic substance.[8]

Dabrowska herself made some statements which can be connected with the above mentioned problem. On the one hand, she claimed that her own main concern in writing was her interest in the element of life:

"So far as I am concerned, I simply wanted to express in that novel my love for the rhythm of life, life which constantly flows and passes by"—Dabrowska said about *Nights and Days* in the interview in *Wiadomosci Literackie* in 1932.[9] At the same time, however, Dabrowska expressed her views on Joseph Conrad's epic qualities which she thought inadequate: "Conrad possesses too little inclination for enjoying the very flowing and passing of life to be a real epic writer, he has too little of contemplative, understanding love, full of compassion for existence as we find it." [10]

The problem, to be sure, is not so simple, and Dabrowska's verdict quoted above is just one side of the picture. Conrad himself claimed an attitude similar to the one which Dabrowska attributes to herself. He, too, as his main concern pronounces his interest in the mysteries of human life. In the "Foreword" to the American edition of his *Short Tales*, Conrad attempts to correct the common view of him as a "writer of the sea."

As a matter of fact I have written of the sea very little, if the pages were counted. It has been the scene, but very seldom the aim of my endeavor. It is too late after all those years; so I will confess here that when I launched my first paper boats in the days of my literary childhood, I aimed at an element as restless, as dangerous, as changeable as the sea, and even more vast; the unappeasable ocean of human life.[11]

Curiously enough this truly epic "confession" came at exactly the same time as Dabrowska's judgment that Conrad lacked the proper epic attitude toward life. Whatever the solution of the problem posed by this conflict of personal views, Dabrowska's pronouncements on the essence of epic writing and on her own goals must be considered as at least partly symptomatic, especially in the light of the many acknowledgments by various critics of her epic talents.

Leo Tolstoy had a few things to say on the matter of the epic style, things that certainly apply in Maria Dabrowska's case. For Tolstoy, the ideal of artistic perfection was a style so natural that it would be completely invisible. This does not mean that he was not concerned with stylistic finesses; on the contrary, the test of "naturalness" for him was the test of careful and successful work; looking at a work of literature, he always asked his three questions: who? what? and how? And the "how?" was in no way less important than who? and what?

Dabrowska's style, from the start, has been praised for just this very quality, for its naturalness, unpretentiousness, clarity, and simplicity. This is especially apparent against the background of the preceding decade in Polish prose when the expressionist styles of such writers as Julius Kaden-Bandrowski, Stefan Zeromski and Zofia Nalkowska (not to speak of such minor authors as J. Woloszynowski or J. Wiktor) developed at times into painful mannerism. In contrast, Dabrowska's natural, "invisible" style was truly refreshing. At the same time, her stylistic means, especially in sketching characteristic individual features, cover a wide range of the most minute nuances.

A good illustration of this point is the scene of Bogumil's proposal to Barbara in the first volume of the novel. Through a series of stylistic contrasts in the speech of these two people, the writer is able to suggest the character and the temperament of each of them, almost without resorting to the method of explicitly telling the reader what these features are supposed to be. The scene consists almost entirely of dialogue parts, in which the author barely intervenes with "staging" remarks. The dialogue reveals all the important differences in the character of Bogumil and Barbara: Bogumil, having once realized his love for Barbara, decides to propose to her before her departure, clarifying the situation once and for all; Barbara, on the other hand, is full of indecision and anxieties, and does not want any clarity in the situation; she does not want to commit herself to Bogumil, yet does not want to lose him by a refusal:

On the last day, almost in the last hour of Miss Ostrzenska's visit in Borek, Niechcic told her how he felt.

It was in the park where they took a walk before her departure for the railroad. Miss Barbara would have given anything for not having to answer—for being excused from this obligation.

—One moment, she finally said, taking a deep breath, one moment. You must think it over, perhaps you are not quite sure if you love me. It seems impossible to me. I don't feel that I deserve it.

—I am sure that I love you, he answered gloomily. But since you say so, it means that I am not agreeable to you, he added in such voice as if he were talking of a death verdict.

—No, it is not that you are not agreeable to me, she said in distress, it is only that it seems to me that we are not . . . that we are not for each other.

—Why not? he asked, trying to overcome the effect which these words had on him. And suddenly he answered himself: Yes, indeed, we are not for each other. You are right to refuse me. You, with your beauty, with your position in the world, deserve a better lot than being tied to the kind of man I am.

—What do you mean? Why? she exclaimed in despair,—but from the house they were calling that it was time to take off. The conversation was interrupted . . .

When Barbara realizes that Bogumil understands her indecisive answers for a refusal and takes him aside in the house in order to improve the impression while still delaying the decision, her "straight" answers become still more chaotic and indecisive:

—I am not refusing you; you misunderstood me. Only there is so little time and I am taken by surprise. It is difficult to talk it over. Listen. They are calling for us!

Indeed, from the veranda, there were shouts: Well, it is enough, young people, enough with secrets!

—Then, let us decide this. If I come here for Christmas, it will mean that everything is all right, that I agree. Or, rather, no. I will write and explain everything in the letter. Or, no . . . you'd better come to Warsaw for All Souls' Day. Or you write, and I will answer. And don't worry. Everything will be all right. Only we have to wait a little while.

Bogumil looked attentively at her and repeated:

—Thank you. All right. I will come. I will write. I will wait.[12]

It is easy to see how the contrast in these two characters is shown by letting them speak in a way which is perfectly conventional and yet, at the same time, completely natural. The phraseology used by each of the interlocutors is quite typical for the situation described, but it is in full agreement with individual character and mood. The author does not make either of them more noble or more romantic than ordinary people; neither does she make them more ridiculous than normal people in situations of this kind, where there is often a note of humor in spite of the romantic mood.

The form of dialogue plays, on the whole, an important role in the novel and toward the end of the work its function increases in proportion to strictly descriptive parts. Of course, here too, as in *People from Yonder,* the impression of direct conversational style is enhanced by the author's frequently resorting to the device of the earlier mentioned reported or narrated speech. In accordance with a natural tendency toward a unity of style it can be easily observed that with the increasing role of dialogues the form of direct speech becomes more aggressive, as it were, and this results in the intermediate device of reported speech. Even such a hybrid as something that could be called "collective interior monologue" can be observed in situations where the author relates the thoughts of the two people at the same time:

For look, how all this thinking: and if . . . perhaps . . . provided that . . . etc., did not help them any. They anticipated, it would seem, all possibilities, and yet they overlooked something important. Life went its own unpredictable course. Where they expected trouble, they now see success. Perhaps it will turn out equally well with little Thomas . . .[13]

"Bogumil is very much inclined to believe this . . ." The relation goes on, unnoticeably changing into the stream of inner thoughts of only one of the two people, and then again returning to the purely narrative form. This free intercourse between the basic narrative structure and the free usage of intermediate structures is a clear sign of Dabrowska's training in the modern technique of novel writing.

At least one more example of this compromise—a compromise carried to such an extreme that it would be impossible to draw the line between the two structures—deserves attention here:

—We are lucky, Niechcic stated gaily. Right after dinner we intended to go and look for you, Mrs. Arkuszowa.

Whereupon Arkuszowa [said] that no, on the contrary, she has been looking for them for a long time.

—She has been looking? why?, Barbara asked when all the greetings and regards were exchanged.

She has been looking, for it turned out that the purchase of the apartment house could be negotiated. Mrs. Arkuszowa did not need any explanations. She was well informed about all the events of the day. She just learned that they were all leaving the office of the notary public, and she ran there first. She does not want them to miss the opportunity, and she advises that they in any case look at the object.

—Then where is this apartment house? Is it far?

—Why should it be far? It's almost here.[14]

It is of course a must in modern literature to give the people from various ethnic, social and regional groups an accent of authenticity by reproducing certain linguistic peculiarities associated with these groups. Dabrowska—as we have seen from her *People from Yonder* (and also from the last line of the above quoted conversation between the Niechcics and the Jewish woman Arkuszowa)—is no exception in this respect. Dabrowska utilizes the method of linguistic characterization consistently, albeit moderately and discretely, with orientation toward the national standard both in the narrative and in the discourse parts. Nevertheless, there are many peasant words and expressions in the speech of the numerous peasants and servants in and around the estates which the Niechcic family occupied during the various period of their life as described in the novel; there are some typical features usually ascribed to the Jews in the speech of Szynszel and Arkuszowa; there are some phonetic and lexical Russianisms in the speech of Orlowicz who is from the Eastern territories, and so forth.

One of the well-known stylistic devices in the poetics of modern realism is the note of irony by means of which the author achieves the effect of distance and objectivity in his relationship to his heroes. The device is especially useful when characters become involved in romantic situations and the author is carried along, suddenly discovering, too late, as it were, that he has been carried too far. Such is the function of the slightly humorous last line in the earlier quoted conversation between Bogumil and Barbara where the hero, after his battle for straightforward answers, gives way to the confused chatter of Miss Ostrzenska and meekly echoes her contradictory statements. This note of irony toward her favorite hero can be heard from Dabrowska on a number of occasions, and, characteristically enough, largely in situations where he might otherwise have appeared too deep or too idealistic or too romantic. In such cases Dabrowska may pull him down, as it were, from his high pedestal; a single word or phrase like the archaic, "Thus spake Bogumil," or, almost mocking, "Watch me making history"—phrases which are out of key with the immediately preceding style—serves the purpose of re-establishing the proper perspective.

In depicting people, Dabrowska uses mostly the indirect method, well-established in the practice of realism, of implying their character by simply letting them talk and act, rather than by telling the reader about them. However, she does not hesitate to resort to this latter method when she apparently finds it more expedient; she even allows herself the old-fashioned writer's convenience—a convenience which in the poetics of modern realism, ever since the time of Maupassant's stories, has been considered a grave "sin"—of omnisciently informing the reader what various people think instead of allowing both the reader and the novel's other protagonists to draw their own conclusions. This, incidentally, is partly connected with the fact that the author does not use any other narrator in this novel; being obliged to narrate for herself, Dabrowska finds it more natural, and, to be sure, more convenient, to inform the reader directly of certain facts and thoughts, then to resort to the polyphonic principle which requires a long chain of witnesses and participants relating only things about which they have first-hand knowledge.

Another of Dabrowska's transgressions against the classical rules of realism are the quite numerous aphoristic passages in which she directly or in a somewhat impersonal form ("it would seem that . . . ," "they say that . . . ," etc.) expresses her views on life and people. It does not mean that she believes in preaching, but she is convinced that a certain amount of reflection behind the events described in a novel is permissible and, indeed, artistically functional.

Speaking of an artist's resort to personal recollections and reflections, Dabrowska has stressed the fact that when she spoke of
the need of a certain contemplative and disinterested distance
from this material in order to achieve the proper aesthetic attitude, she did not mean that such an attitude should be passive
and indifferent. On the contrary, for her this attitude is active, it
does not prevent the writer's active participation in the process of
life. This explains why Dabrowska considers a writer's personal
recollections so important in artistic work, and this is probably the
reason for her freedom in interweaving "objective" realistic presentation with personal thoughts which are the sum of her experience and her convictions.

In defending a writers' freedom in his choice of the various
means of artistic composition and in blending several of them together, Dabrowska points to Marcel Proust's method of incorpo-
rating his very personal psychological and philosophical experience in the stream of the narrative and yet not making the whole
work less acceptable as a work of art. Even in an epic work, while
recognizing the need for perspective and objectivity, and while
practicing such stylistic devices as the above mentioned device of
irony which serve this purpose in modern literature, Dabrowska
does not recognize the demand for the writer's complete neutral-
ity in presenting his heroes. On the contrary, she is of the opinion
that the author should bear full responsibility for the world which
he creates. She also points out that the sum of the author's ideals is
automatically present to a higher or lesser degree in the people of
this world. Her comment on the problem of a possible "guiding
thought" in her novel may be recalled here:

I am deeply convinced that if I myself—consciously or unconsciously—possess a guiding idea in life, character, and spiritual attitude toward the world, all this will unavoidably find its artistic reflection in the content of my work.[15]

The main secret of Dabrowska's style seems to be the ability to
incorporate the comments, the aphorisms, the innumerable stylistic devices into the main stream of the narrative in such a way
that the "seams" with which these parts are held together are al-

most invisible. According to the context, the author's remarks are introduced by a connecting word or phrase so that they appear as an organic part of the description or conversation or whatever form this context has. Again the term "natural style" must be repeated. Dabrowska certainly fits Pascal's formula, taken as motto of this chapter: "quand on voit le style naturel, on est tout étonné: car on s'attendait de voir un auteur, et on trouve un homme."

A few examples of Dabrowska's reflection discreetly but openly incorporated in the story, now as author's comment, now as the thoughts of one of the heroes, may be worth pointing out here.

At one point the thoughts of a person, Michaeline Ostrzenska, develop into a comment about her mentality, which in turn acquires a general character of reflection on human rationalization of instincts and desires:

And Aunt Michaeline was nevertheless a little angry with her brother-in-law. For, she seriously believed and wished that Anselm's enterprise be of a great social significance. Whatever purpose one serves, a human being wants to believe that he works for a great lasting goal.

It is hard to tell what is more real: deeds motivated by egoistic reasons, or the soul's longing which is trying to cover them with ideals and elevate them to the dignity of duty.[16]

On another occasion we see how Barbara's reflections merge imperceptibly into the author's own:

Barbara decided not to touch lace-making any more. She was looking forward to other more active spiritual pleasures, and although it was only expectation, even the thought of these pleasures made the triviality of everyday living more bearable. For the feeling that we have something to look forward to, something that we imagine real, transforms into reality what seemed earlier only a shadow of reality.[17]

Or finally, the author's "philosophical" reflections can be observed in Barbara's thoughts:

Finally she abandoned these thoughts since they did not seem to lead anywhere. Apparently it must be so among the people: aversion and attachment, estrangement and community; none of these feelings are lost forever and fill one's heart entirely; without one's knowing when, one of these feelings turns into another . . .[18]

Speaking of the various stylistic devices, it may be also noted that Dabrowska frequently uses a device especially popular during the period of symbolism, namely the inclusion of nature imagery in the rhythm of events and in the thoughts of characters so as to intensify their experience and stress their mood at a particular moment. Of course, this nature background, as it has always been in lyric poetry, can either harmonize or contrast with the mood of persons.

So, for example, in a moment of Bogumil's depression and indecision when he moves toward an unpleasant decisive talk with his assistant, Katelba:

He lit a cigarette and went out. Outside of the house he stopped and looked upwards. On his face he felt innumerable touches of drizzle. Thick darkness covered the sky.
—Three-day rain—he thought, walking toward the farm-workers' quarters. He was oppressed by the thought that he was going to face one of those things in which there is no established pattern of solution, no model of action, no indication of what might prove a practical and moral victory . . .[19]

To be sure, this mode of associating human emotions with phenomena of nature is so common that in many literary works we can encounter scenes almost identical to the one quoted above. In Thomas Mann's *Buddenbrooks*, for example, there is an almost identical passage at the end of the first part, where the frustrations of the people are harmonized with the image of a house submerged in darkness:

Soon the rambling old house lay wrapped in darkness and silence. Hopes, fears, and ambitions all slumbered while the rain fell and the autumn wind whistled around gables and street corners.[20]

Perhaps it should be remarked that in Thomas Mann's work the various stylistic devices are more harmonized; his method is more

[76]

disciplined and his work is more consistent and orderly than the freely flowing narrative of Dabrowska's epos.

It has been stressed that the novel *Nights and Days* can be analyzed from various points of view in regard to the various interrelated motifs around which the "story" circles. Thus we have the motif of two radically different characters, brought together in marital life to face a changing world and to react to these changes according to their basic characters; closely connected with this is the theme of "love without a partner." Then there is the wider social problem of the changing economic conditions of a whole class and a still wider theme of the world's changing intellectual and political climate, represented by the old concept of peaceful nineteenth century evolutionism giving way to the turbulence of revolution and the preparation for the World War. At the same time we have the theme of two generations and their intricate relationships against the background of all these changes.

At all times we observe the intricate, yet not tangled, interplay of all these themes. The composition of the work, like most other epic works, is based on the principle of parallelism in the fates of individual heroes and the collective life of their society. These two levels, the individual and the collective, are, of course, inseparable; the individual fates illuminate the changes in the collective life, and the larger events, as, for example, the revolutionary movement, influence the course of events in the individual fates of the respective heroes.

The main common denominator of all these themes is the universal theme of human beings constantly seeking their place in life, constantly striving for some kind of future, constantly moving on the paths of their individual lives, paths which now parallel, now intersect, the road of their society, a road which hardly ever leads them where they think they are going, but which nevertheless always leads them eventually toward their human destiny.

This is one of the reasons why Dabrowska does not especially care for the label *roman fleuve*, sometimes given her work in critical literature, especially in the way some writers have elaborated on this term, suggesting that the "river" of life depicted in her novel could just as well go on much longer, almost without an end. In this regard, Dabrowska has overcome her modesty to remark, somewhat ironically, that even a river must have its eventual end in the ocean, pointing out that, after all, the course of her main theme is carried to its logical end. Bogumil's death and Barbara's attainment of peace of mind in losing all material security and most of her previous illusions and ambitions closes both the main individual theme of the two personalities and also the social theme of people moving from one social group to another.

CHAPTER 4

The Test of Integrity: The Morning Star

"Les révolutions changent tout,
sauf le coeur humain."

Pascal

I Signs of Life

AFTER the completion of the big novel cycle *Nights and Days,*
Dabrowska on the one hand returns to the form of the short
story and, on the other, tries her hand in the dramatic genre. In
1938 she published a new volume of short stories, entitled *Signs of
Life (Znaki zycia),* and shortly thereafter, in 1939, she finished
her first dramatic work, *The Orphan Genius (Geniusz sierocy).* At
the same time Dabrowska was very active both in the field of
literary criticism and also as a publicist of steadily growing moral
authority, even though her views were somewhat too utopian to
be of any direct practical value.

The collection of short stories entitled *Signs of Life* is characterized largely by the features which have been observed in *People
from Yonder.* Thus we see how the author oscillates in her narrative form between the traditional straightforward relation of facts
and observations, and the more modernistic mode of mixing various levels and directions of plot and point of view in order to
illuminate various aspects of human character and human reactions to situations which are mostly rather ordinary and hardly
amount to the established idea of a "plot."

The first story, "Father Philip," is an example of a rather traditional technique of short-story pattern based on an inner struggle
between ideal and reality. The actual plot here is the frequently
utilized theme of conflict between a Catholic priest's vocation
with its vows of purity and the reality of worldly temptations and
indulgences, even including sexual relationship with a woman.
In Polish literature this theme was introduced earlier, during the
period of Symbolism, in a dramatic work by Stanislaw Wyspian-

ski. This was *The Curse* (*Klatwa,* 1899), a work in which the problem was presented from the point of view of classical tragedy as epitomized in *King Oedipus.*

Dabrowska does not hesitate to take up this touchy theme, but with her characteristic life-affirmative attitude she presents her vision as one of those "age-old" moral questions which, in her opinion, art should always take up and present in the light of experience, as a projection for the future of new generations for which no situation should be regarded as absolutely hopeless. The basic problem in Dabrowska's story is not so much the problem of the priest's sin and his deserved punishment, but the problem of charity, the problem of man's supreme obligation to possess compassion and understanding for other human beings. Dabrowska's thesis in this story is the conviction that although sin is always sin, there is something far worse, namely the lack of charity between human beings.

The synthesis of these thoughts is achieved in a scene where Father Philip, having completed his personal reckoning of sins, gets to the outline of his last sermon, "the first real sermon" in his life:

"And if it seems to you," he writes, "that you have chosen the wrong occupation, that you will not persevere in your calling, remember that there is in the world one occupation, only one calling—to be good to another human being."

He crosses this out and begins anew:

"To count one's sins, this is not life, it is decay. There is only one life and one calling: to help people. The world moves ahead not through the fulfilling of law, but through good deeds . . ."

This seems to him too difficult for the people to understand, and not even entirely clear to himself. Again he crosses it out and takes another sheet:

"Whoever you are, priest, government employee or peasant, you will accomplish nothing and fail to reach God without love for man. For there is only one calling . . . one road to salvation. . ." [1]

Like Dionysius in *People from Yonder,* and like Bogumil Niechcic in *Nights and Days,* the old priest is able to express his deepest thoughts only in a moment of an unusual state of mind; he, like Bogumil Niechcic, is not a very communicative man, and not of a very reflective nature. For him too there is a rare light of revelation just before his tragic end.

Other stories of this collection contain less typical short-story plot material. Instead, the psychological penetration so typical of Dabrowska is frequently encountered. There are elements of keen realistic observation of life and elements of serious reflection on the reaction of various characters in different situations, both usual and unique. Some of the characters and situations encountered are very typical, but even then, as for example in the story, "Miss Winczewska" ("Panna Winczewska"), the individual features are drawn with such a degree of vividness that the characters stand out as individuals. The story is a precise, almost clinical analysis of character and situation and is obviously based on the author's long personal experience with professional and educational organizations. The routine of work in a small library is shown here with all its technical details, and the confrontation of two characters with two different attitudes toward work keeps the reader in suspense, in spite of the fact that there is no classical plot, no real short-story intrigue. It is a psychological study, artistically organized into a finished unit.

Actually, it is possible to speak of a plot here, but not plot in the common meaning of the word. There is an internal psychological development, perhaps less dramatic than is usually encountered in a story of intrigue, but nevertheless fascinating as a struggle within an individual, a struggle between emotional and rational elements, a struggle in which the intricate nature of human relations is reflected with the suggestive power of a true picture. It is surprising to observe how this seemingly detached clinical study of human character turns into a classical "little tragedy" in which all the ingredients of a dramatic situation are potentially present, even though they never come completely to the fore. The climax of the story is the scene in which the rational appraisal of the qualities of Miss Winczewska by her superior, the head of the library, clashes with a sudden attainment of human contact between the two people, a realization that the professional competence is not the only level on which their relationship operates.

There is something of Chekhov's depth of penetration into the life of ordinary people in this story, and here, as in the case of Jens Peter Jacobsen, a reflection can be made that Dabrowska's work as Chekhov's translator[2] was not a matter of accident, but the result of a certain artistic and intellectual affinity.

In another story, "A Piece of Glass" ("Szkielko"), we find a different approach to human problems. In contrast to the previous story where the stress was put on typical, ordinary situations, and typical, normal decisions, we find here a demonstration of the individual reaction of a less ordinary person—member of the Polish underground movement—to a situation which, though not unique, is nevertheless more unusual than the situation of Miss Winczewska. The theme of the story is, again, a psychological one: the hero finds himself in prison and faces the possibility of compromising his dignity should he prove unable to withstand pressure and perhaps even physical torture, thus betraying the organization. In this situation a small, trivial item—a piece of glass accidentally discovered in the cell—acquires the proportions of a symbol, the symbol of ultimate solution, a possible instrument of suicide. This device of making a small, insignificant piece of reality the central structural point of a story (or a dramatic work) is well-known in literature. Here, as in many other works, Dabrowska blends successfully the familiar features with her own unmistakable technique in sketching an individual human character and the circumstances in which this character has to face a crisis. It should be pointed out that in the case of this story, as in some other cases in Dabrowska's work, we have an example of an auto-reminiscence. The situation constituting the basic motif here was also utilized by the author in her novel, *Nights and Days,* in one of the episodes which Marcin Sniadowski relates to Agnieszka.

The two remaining stories in the volume, "A Trifle" ("Drobiazg") and "Octavia" ("Oktawia"), seem somewhat accidental, but then, according to an introductory statement, Dabrowska's artistic goal here is almost directly opposed to the internal unity she achieved in *People from Yonder.* She conceived each one of the stories in this volume as a kind of "musical étude." In each story the artist's emphasis is on demonstrating her ability "to build up a short work without adhering to the established rules of the classical short story." [3] "A Trifle" is the psychological study of a woman who is passing beyond her youth and faces the problem of remaining unmarried. As in the case of "A Piece of Glass," the motif belongs to the circle of *Nights and Days;* Dabrowska simply develops one of the numerous secondary themes, giving a separate psychological sketch of one of the minor figures in the novel, Oktawia Kociellowna. Another woman of the same first name is the subject of the story entitled "Octavia." Here the effect of a complete artistic unity is achieved by an accumulation of realistic details as reflected in the reactions of a sensitive individual.

As was indicated in the preface to this study, stress has been put primarily on Dabrowska's narrative prose. Her dramatic, critical, and journalistic production is only touched upon to the extent that it contains material relevant to this main stream of artistic production. It could be argued, to be sure, that the two dramatic works written by Dabrowska should be placed on the same level with her short stories and with her novel cycle. However, it is the opinion of this writer that Dabrowska's plays are closer to her work as a publicist and are not organically related to the main stream of her creative work. Of course, it is perfectly true, on the other hand, that in her journalistic work Dabrowska is often more of a writer than a politician. One of the best illustrations of this fact is her political article in protest against the political climate in prewar Poland, "On the Difficult Road" ("Na ciezkiej drodze"), published in the weekly, *Wiadomosci Literackie* (No. 4, 1931), and reprinted in the Socialist daily, *Naprzod* (Nos. 18, 20, 23, 24, 1931). The most effective part of this article is an extended metaphor in which the historical figure of the famous sixteenth century Chancellor Jan Zamoyski is used as a contrastive symbol to the collective body of the political group governing Poland after J. Pilsudski's military coup d'état of 1926. This powerful metaphor is based on the historical testimony that when a rebellious magnate, Samuel Zborowski, was condemned to death by Zamoyski, the Chancellor begged the prisoner's forgiveness as he was led to the place of execution. This scene, which is the climax in Slowacki's drama, is echoed with biting irony in Dabrowska's essay:

Our contemporary Jan Zamoyski, represented by the members of the pro-government party, was *laughing* [stressed by Dabrowska. Z. F.] when the issue of Brześć was raised in the Parliament. And this indecent laughter will long resound in Poland, but nobody will feel like laughing from it.[4]

In Dabrowska's dramatic works a similar device is used, but in reverse: contemporary problems are introduced into this literary form in the guise of historical motifs.

II *Out of the Ruins*

The horrors of war, the occupation, the desperate Warsaw uprising and the destruction of the city—all these tragic events found only fragmentary reflection in Dabrowska's literary production. Nevertheless, in some of her works echoes of this period, filtered through the prism of calm reflection from the perspective of postwar reality, can be heard. In most cases, the main point of view of these problems is, again, one of those same "age-old truths" of which Dabrowska spoke in her earlier works; the main concern is human heart, human destiny, human being as a creature of "feelings and thoughts."

Dabrowska spent the entire war period in Warsaw, the city which had been her permanent residence ever since 1917. As a Polish writer and as a member of the intelligentsia she was deprived of any means of support and was able to survive mainly by help from the cooperative institutions, some of which were still allowed to operate as vital to the economic life of the occupied territories. Dabrowska participated in underground cultural and educational activities; she lectured, taught, attended meetings and discussions, had to struggle for survival—avoiding German patrols, standing in lines for bread or meat, trying not to miss the last streetcar before the police curfew, and trying to get news about the military and political situation.

There was not much time or opportunity for literary work under these circumstances. Dabrowska started a novel based on her observations of life under the occupation, but only three parts of this projected work were completed after the war and published in her *Selected Works* (*Pisma wybrane*, Vol. I, Warsaw, 1956). These fragments are "On a Beautiful Summer Morning" ("W piekny letni poranek"), "And Now Let Us Have a Drink" ("A teraz napijmy sie") and "A Stupid Story" ("Glupia historia").

Direct personal reactions to the war on the part of Dabrowska are not numerous, and they are very discreet, consciously devoid of dramatic effects. Only on a few occasions does she allow her emotions to come to the fore in one or another eruption of lyricism and pathos. A notable example of this is her return in February, 1945 to the ruins of Warsaw, which she had left a few months earlier, chased away with the other civilians by the German troops after the insurrection was quelled. "My First Journey to Warsaw" ("Moja pierwsza wedrowka do Warszawy"), written in February, 1945, was published in *Warszawa* (Nos. 1–2 and 3, 1946) and later incorporated as the first story in the volume, *The Morning Star* (*Gwiazda Zaranna*, Warsaw, 1955), under a changed title, "A Pilgrimage to Warsaw" ("Pielgrzymka do Warszawy"). From this story and from a fragment entitled "A Change Came O'er the Scenes of My Dream" ("Tu zaszla zmiana"), which was also included in *The Morning Star,* it is possible to reconstruct some of the writer's personal experiences during the war and some of her thoughts and experiences immediately after the war, when she and her compatriots faced on the one hand the problem of "returning to life," restoring what they had lost, and, on the other, the problem of facing a new political system in their country, a system which quite radically changed many of the things they looked for among the ruins of their houses, among the remnants of their private and collective pasts.

III   *The Test of Integrity*

It was not easy for a writer of Dabrowska's ideological outlook to find her way under conditions of political, ideological and economic change, and under conditions in which art was quickly subordinated to the demands of the official program of Socialist Realism.

While the still chaotic conditions of the first years after the war left some room for searching analyses and experimentation with various concepts of art, the lines of Socialist Realism gradually became more rigid as the only acceptable method, and artists had either to submit, at least in part, to the principles of this doctrine or remain silent.

The majority of works of literature published immediately after the war had been written during the war years. Some writers, to be sure, were quick in their attempts to catch up with postwar political changes, but these attempts were limited mostly to the negative aspects of the program, i.e., to a critique of prewar reality; consequently, they can be regarded as a continuation of "Critical Realism" rather than manifestations of Socialist Realism which for some time remained rather little known in Poland. There were few critics and still fewer writers who were familiar with all the implications of Marxism in art, and thus the proclamations of the new principles seldom went beyond the rephrasing of basic Soviet slogans. Gradually, a more articulate group of people, which gathered around the weekly, *Smithy* (*Kuznica*), tried to formulate some more tangible principles of the new approach to art. At the same time, however, political control of art directed from above, i.e., dictated by the Party, put a stop to free discussion of these matters. In 1949 the doctrine of Socialist Realism was "recommended" at a meeting of the Polish Writers Union, and in 1950 it was officially proclaimed the only method of writing to be supported and, indeed, to be tolerated, in the Polish People's Republic. In practice, to be sure, this method amounted to not much more than the "correctly" oriented presentation of reality, i.e., a presentation in which aspects associated with the new socialist system, with its stress on the value of the collective, would appear constructive and dynamic, while elements opposed to socialism, elements of individualism, would breathe decay and stagnation.[5]

After what has been said about Dabrowska's aesthetic and ideological beliefs, it is easy to see why she could not be the type of writer who would fulfill this "social assignment." She could not but remain faithful to the ideals expressed in her earlier works, ideals among which one of the most important was the conviction that an individual's rights are the most sacred thing in this life.

Quite naturally, in the general re-evaluation of literary values that took place during the so-called Stalinist period—the period which was later somewhat euphemistically called "the period of mistakes and vitiations"—Dabrowska's works were often attacked for their ideological inadequacies from the point of view of the premises of Socialist Realism.

Obviously, then, it was not easy for Maria Dabrowska to continue her creative work. Fortunately, her artistic and moral stature was such that these attacks did not hurt her to any great extent. On the contrary, literary statistics show that Dabrowska, together with such classic writers as Sienkiewicz, Prus, and Orzeszkowa, was one of the most popular writers. The fact that Dabrowska's works were not re-published more frequently resulted,

of course, from the growing political control of publishing activity
—at that time works not written in the spirit of Socialist Realism
were not promoted. Even despite this unfavorable situation there
were several new editions of *People from Yonder* and *Nights and
Days* because the demand was so great. Of course, after the par-
tial change of official policy in 1956, there came many more editions of Dabrowska's works than during the decade 1945–1955,
when, not unlike some of the Russian writers, notably Boris Pasternak, Dabrowska devoted herself chiefly to translations. Her essays on Polish and foreign literature were eventually published
under the title, "Thoughts on Problems and People" ("Mysli o
sprawach i ludziach"), but not until 1956, i.e., after the so-called
"Polish October."

Being a creative writer, however, Dabrowska could not keep
silent for too long. Even during the time when official policy was
still rather rigid, despite certain signs of ferment which could be
seen among Polish intellectuals, Dabrowska decided to publish a
volume of stories which she entitled *The Morning Star* (*Gwiazda
zaranna*). Obviously, under the circumstances some kind of
compromise with the principles of Socialist Realism, especially in
writing on contemporary themes, was unavoidable. Dabrowska
has always had enough faith in human values to be able and will-
ing to see the necessity of such a compromise. She always supported ideas of progress, education, better living and housing conditions for the poorer peasants and workers, and in this respect
there were certain aspects of the new postwar reality in which she
was able to find nourishment for optimism. Thus, the vision of
reality she was able to give in some of her stories could be considered constructive not only from her individual, but also from the
official point of view. This was an honest compromise, a compromise without humiliation, a stand which perhaps required more
courage than passive silent disapproval. Dabrowska did not want
to be one of the "internal émigrés," she wanted to share the life
and responsibilities of her countrymen, and as an artist she did it
by giving expression to her stand in a literary work. She did not
change her cardinal belief in the sanctity of the individual and her
firm conviction that human ideals cannot be governed by regula-
tions. Indeed, at the very time when Polish writers were very per-
suasively instructed in the canons of Socialist Realism—during the

meeting of the Polish Writers' Union in Szczecin in 1949—Dabrowska did not hesitate to express her views on these problems in her talks on literature given on several occasions in a series of "Conversations of Writers with Their Readers":

Writers should express in their works the surrounding reality. Moreover, they should praise this reality, depicting the achievements and the strong, positive men who were able to carry out these successful enterprises. We read about it in the literary press, we hear about it in public speeches, we learn about it from the radio.

So began Dabrowska's analysis of the official recommendations for writers. She spoke of these problems in a wide context, in historical perspective, but there could not have been any doubt that her historical sketch included official recommendations for the Polish writers:

The demands that a writer should write only on contemporary themes[6] can have various reasons, and their character and results can vary. They can be a negative or a positive phenomenon.

As a negative phenomenon "from our viewpoint," Dabrowska cites two instances from the past, the period of the Roman Empire and the time of Louis XIV. However, her characterization of these negative aspects in the official policy of that time must have sounded strangely familiar to her Polish audience of the 'forties:

At the time of Augustus, Trajan, or Nero, writers were obliged to depict all the official triumphs of the state and its rulers. Indeed, even the very absence of a writer at the imperial celebrations was regarded as disloyalty toward the state . . .[7]

On another occasion, two years earlier, Dabrowska touched indirectly and in a much more veiled form on basically the same problem, the problem of the individual's and the people's right to follow the independent course often dictated more by irrational instinct than by reason. In a review article (*Warszawa*, No. 5,

1947) on the occasion of a scholarly book, *Peasants as Defenders of Poland's Independence During the Deluge*[8] by a historian, Stanislaw Szczotka, Dabrowska comes out with the following reflections:

. . . And so a doubt arises as to whether all this splendid partisan struggle of our peasants and Czarniecki against the Swedes was not perhaps at the same time a struggle against the elements of progress which desired to reform Poland. . . . And yet . . . condemning all the excesses, we must conclude that the right was on the side of the peasants who pitilessly chased away the Swedes and punished their adherents. And as for those who took the side of the Swedes, even though there were among them people with the progressive intention of bettering their country, they had to find themselves in conflict with the majority of the people who desired to remain faithful to freedom and independence. Both sides made mistakes, but the mistake of the enlightened "traitors" was much greater than the mistake of the simple, crude "defenders" . . .[9]

IV   The Morning Star

When Dabrowska's volume, *The Morning Star,* appeared, it proved a true artistic and moral triumph for Poland's most cherished and respected writer. It became a literary sensation of unequalled proportions, literally selling out within a few hours after it reached the country's bookstores.

Applying a technique similar to her earlier stories, blending authentic recollections and observations with motifs of pure fiction, Dabrowska created a book which is an artistically finished whole, a book in which, in spite of the fragmentary character of the various stories, there unveils a broad panorama of the tragedy of war and the reality of postwar life with its turns and conflcts, serious problems and everyday worries and joys, tragedies and hopes. In short, the work proved to be the "nights and days" of the Polish people as the author saw them from the perspective of her personal experience, and from her observation of the collective life of the early postwar years. The sharp realism of detailed observations and personal evperiences is, as usually can be expected in Dabrowska's works, permeated by the author's philosophy, her affirmative outlook on life, both past and present. Her philosophical comments are no revelations, but they always contain a good deal of honest, thoughtful penetration into the deeper significance of a particular phenomenon.

A nightmarish pilgrimage through the ruins of Warsaw, her city, destroyed by the Germans in revenge for the uprising, is described with the great vividness of a person who is not only an eyewitness, but who is an integral part of the depicted world:

I walk through the terrible canyon of the destroyed Nowy Swiat Street toward the Trzech Krzyzy Square. Melting snow, mud, jagged walls of the dead houses; through the holes of windows one can see the mild grey sky and the rubble inside. Big letters on the walls: No mines. Defused on such and such date. Or: Mines! [10]

And in the midst of all the destruction, signs of life which fill the author with optimism, even if it is at first the same somewhat fatalistic optimism which we witnessed in "The Triumph of Dionysius":

Out of the depth of feelings there rises a strange kind of enthusiasm which we experience at the time when we reach the bottom of disaster, and the only thing left is to get the courage and move upwards.[11]

Out of these scattered realistic fragments and philosophical reflections emerges a vision of a world in which, in the midst of ruins, the fetor of death, misery and deprivation, there beats a pulse of life, a throbbing human heart. Pathos blends with comedy in some of the observed scenes and many a trivial detail leads to a deeper thought.

Thus, for example, "Pilgrimage to Warsaw" ends with a scene in which somebody notices a louse on the author's coat:

Oh well, war . . . migration of people . . . lice. It is nothing. We must have an ocean of patience and persistence in difficulties to get where time is calling us.[12]

At the same time there are some reflections of a more melancholy character, reflections with a universal note:

Humanity arranged for itself a monstrous loss of time. Enthusiasm which could have produced the most splendid spiritual and material achievements burns here into a moment of joy on account of a trifle, a memento of the past dug out of the rubble . . .[13]

In most of the stories in this volume, elements of reality and the personal recollections of the author blend together. These involve mostly such well-known motifs as graves of friends and relatives, loss of all worldly possessions including the roof overhead, half-nomadic life, hospitality of friends and strangers, greediness and theft of others, lack of food, lack of sanitation, lack of transportation, willingness to live. All this is narrated with a note of personal experience and authenticity, but with epic calmness, free of pathos and sentimentalism, though not deprived of a thoughtful philosophical assessment. The most personal stories are: "A Night Meeting" ("Nocne spotkanie") which describes the author's encounter with some Soviet soldiers on a train; and "A Change Came O'er the Scenes of My Dream" ("Tu zaszla zmiana")—a masterful cinematic presentation of stages in the changing scenery seen from the window of the writer's study. As in a motion picture, the changing scenery reveals, one after another, various aspects of the tragic, merciless course of war and occupation, with elements of tragedy, heroism, banality, and the signs of optimism so usual with Dabrowska.

The first scene of "A Change Came O'er the Scenes of My Dream" is a prewar picture of an idyllic house with a little enclosed yard. In the second scene—in September, 1939—the roof of the house is partially blown away by German bombs and the scene is extended, allowing a view of two other houses beyond. In the next scene—the Warsaw Uprising of 1944—the little enclosed yard becomes a graveyard for the dead insurgents; the civilians must leave. Then it is February, 1945. The houses are no more than jagged walls and there are more graves in the yard; a schoolhouse nearby is being restored and children are playing among the graves. One day, after a remark by the writer, the children tidy up the neglected cemetery, bring flowers, frame the graves with stones; the temporary cemetery is kept in order for some time after. But one day, again the scenery changes. The graves are exhumed by a special brigade, and the lot is converted into playgrounds for the school-children. The scenario ends with an optimistic prediction that perhaps one day there will again be a green yard among modern new apartment houses for people who will work for the bright future of their country.

Motifs concerning the writer's personal hardships during this period are almost absent in the stories. Only from certain scant details scattered here and there in the volume can we reconstruct the pattern of her life, a life which must have been much the same as that of the majority of her compatriots. There is a reference to her being forced to leave her home temporarily and seek harbor elsewhere while the house was put under German surveillance. There is another reference to a broken arm, to her sister's death, and to many common everyday details from the war period, but the author's main concern is not with herself.

V   A Noble Compromise

The last two stories in the volume occupy a different position. The stories, "The Third Autumn" ("Trzecia jesien") and "A village Wedding" ("Na wsi wesele"), both describing the postwar reality, constitute a counter-balance to the retrospective stories in the first part of the book. They are both considerably longer and they occupy more space than the other seven stories together. "A Village Wedding," a story eighty pages long, must be especially treated as a separate unit, as a work which has some features of a short novel.

To understand these two stories, the problem of the writer's ideological position must be discussed briefly. As was remarked at the beginning of the chapter, Dabrowska's ideals were based on her faith in the value of the individual. One of the problems for her in the postwar period was the question of retaining and voicing that faith in the face of the strong official emphasis on the collective. This was the same conflict as the one discernible in Soviet literature of the so-called Thaw period, and Dabrowska's stand in this respect is not unlike that taken by such Soviet writers as, especially, Vladimir Dudintsev in his novel, Not by Bread Alone.

A good illustration of Dabrowska's thoughts on this problem is her polemic-writing on the subject of Joseph Conrad and his views on human destiny. When in the monthly, *Tworczosc* (*Creative Writing*) No. 2, 1945, the critic Jan Kott attacked Conrad's "morality" from a Marxist position, Dabrowska came to the defense of Conrad's ideals. In an article, "On Conrad's Concept of Faithfulness," followed by an additional "Random Note on J. Kott's Essay," published in *Warszawa*, Dabrowska formulated some of the basic principles underlying the conflicting views of the individual versus the collective. Matching Conrad's vision of the world, according to which "the destiny of the collective is determined by the morality of concrete individuals," against the Marxist view promoted by Kott that "the morality of the individual is determined by the morality of the collective," Dabrowska quite extensively discusses the chances of a compromise between these attitudes in an exposé that amounts to an exercise of sorts in dialectics:

The tragedy in each of these two attitudes begins where the other one fails. We saw, during the last six years, people who took their own lives because even their highest personal morality was unable to prevent the evil which flooded the world on the order of a well-organized collective. And we saw crowds of people brought up in the seemingly best school of collective life, who were unable to produce even the most elementary features of personal human decency, once they found themselves outside of the rigid norms of their milieu. They were not taught to care for their inner rectitude. The way to discharge this tragic conflict would be in a compromise between these two attitudes. Life, in order to move forward, always needs a compromise between extreme attitudes. There are compromises that are fair and just, that are beneficial for life and cleanse it, and there are compromises that are disgraceful, that poison the atmosphere and give birth to new more and more insoluble conflicts. But even the most honest and wise compromise will not discharge all the tragedy in this area. For it is not always and not everywhere that a compromise is applicable.[14]

As can be seen, Dabrowska's stand is clear and firm. She recognizes the necessity and the value of a compromise, but she is fully aware of the fact that there are limits beyond which one cannot go without losing integrity. In the conflict between the two philosophies as outlined in the above quotation, Dabrowska stands clearly on the side of those for whom an individual, a human being, is an absolute value. For her, as for Conrad, an individual is the proverbial tree which should not be lost from sight for the sake of the forest.

The best artistic expression of these thoughts is the story, "The Third Autumn." There is a strong, persistent note of individualism in this story, a firm faith in the individual's right to his own life and to his own convictions. The hero of the story, Klemens Lohojski, is an individual who is outside the collective. He is an oddball, according to some people, a "senile bum" to others. Yet, somehow, this "crazy," "extravagant," "non-organized" individual, without any steady job, can make himself helpful and useful to almost everybody he encounters on his way, can bring happiness and joy to many, even to those who, according to the law of the collective, should be much happier than he is. Lohojski carries on a persistent, lonely fight for the right to obtain a garden plot where he can grow flowers and vegetables. This is more than a hobby, it is his passion, and while he fights for his own plot, he makes miracles with planting for other people. There is an undercurrent of the struggle between the two philosophies discussed above. The individual in this story is not an enemy of the collective, but he fights for his right to do things in his own way, to be useful to others in a different way from that prescribed by the official program. In this he strongly resembles the inventor, Lopatkin, in Dudintsev's *Not by Bread Alone*.

You are not starting from the right end [says the janitor, referring to Lohojski's unsuccessful attempts at obtaining a garden plot]. Being merely a man is not enough. You have to have your papers in order, and you simply must find a permanent job first. Then there will be health insurance, garden plot, everything.[15]

And yet, this crazy, idealistic fight ends with a final victory. As in the case of *Not by Bread Alone*, the solution of the plot is found in a compromise; the collective eventually gives way and gives its approval to the ideas of the persistent individual. In this way the integrity of the individual is preserved and the ultimate wisdom of the system based on the dictates of the collective is not compromised.

The Russian inventor, Lopatkin, although he was discouraged

and persecuted by the officials in power, finally succeeds in putting his idea through to the highest instance and, of course, according to the principles of Socialist Realism, this highest instance cannot be wrong. His victory is, at the same time, the victory of the Party.

Klemens Lohojski in "The Third Autumn" wins the collective's sanction for his actually illegal work on someone else's garden plot. Not only does he win everybody's love and respect, but he is awarded an official prize for his inventive methods in growing melons. Here too, the collective can be said to be proven right and wise.

The compromise is based on the possibility of putting the emphasis on either the one or the other side of the issue. The individual values can be said to have been saved by the collective; the collective can be said to have saved its face by giving way to the individual. The most objective suggestion may be that what actually should not happen within the frame of reference of the rigid principles of Socialist Realism, may be possible if the collective makes a few concessions for a somewhat greater individual freedom. Of course, as was the case with Dabrowska's earlier ideological intervention, in "The Crossroads," her compromise stand could not be entirely satisfactory to any one group. There were those, especially in Polish official circles, who thought that she went too far in speaking up for individual rights. And there were others, especially among the opposition within Poland and also in émigré circles in the West, who felt that she did not show enough resistance to the official course in Poland.[16]

Looking at the whole situation from an historical perspective, it seems that Dabrowska's compromise solution was the maximum of what was possible at the time of the writing of the story. Its first publication was in the weekly, *Nowa Kultura,* No. 14, 1954. To have said so much about the sacred rights of the individual at a time when the absolute supremacy of the Socialist collective was being officially proclaimed as the only correct, constructive theme in literature, was a most unique artistic and moral triumph, a triumph which only an artist of Maria Dabrowska's stature and integrity could have achieved.

To return once more to Dabrowska's polemics with the critic,

paper for the publishing of books and periodicals. The result was that a split arose in the Polish Writers Association. A number of writers signed a politically motivated manifesto of loyalty and support of the government. However, when at the meeting of the Warsaw chapter of the Association held on June 12, 1964, Maria Dabrowska, who was one of the 34 signers of the original protest, defended their stand and their moral right to do what they had done, she was rewarded by applause from all fellow-writers—both those who had signed the original petition and those who had later signed an "anti-protest" expressing their support of the government policy. This unique "unity in contradiction"—to use the Hegelian term—is one of those rare unpredictable instances which defy logic, but which nevertheless, do happen, even outside of fiction. In this incident taken from real life, as in her fiction, in the story of Klemens Lohojski, Dabrowska's faith in man, in the integrity of the human heart, proved stronger than the dictates of Socialist Realism. She stood forth and was honored as a great artist and as a person loved and respected both by those who shared her convictions and by those who opposed them. This was indeed a rewarding moment in the career of the aging and ailing writer.[18]

CHAPTER 5

Dabrowska in Literary Criticism

I Reception at Home

WHEN, in 1923, Maria Dabrowska was awarded the Publishers' Prize for her volume, *The Smile of Childhood,* she was virtually unknown to readers in Poland, and, as she herself later recalled, the reaction in most cases was the surprised question: Who is she? Two years later Dabrowska again surprised the reading public with her volume, *People from Yonder,* which met with a generally enthusiastic reception. With a few exceptions, critics did not hesitate to call Dabrowska a great talent.

The first more substantial, and indeed in many ways pioneer, study was written by Karol W. Zawodzinski. Immediately after the appearance of the first volume of *Nights and Days,* this sensitive critic, educated in the tradition of modern Western and Russian poetry and prose and well versed in the theory and practice of the so-called formal school of literary criticism in Russia, published two long chapters in the monthly *Contemporary Review* (*Przeglad wspolczesny*) under the common title, "Maria Dabrowska. The Literary Significance of Her Work." [1] Zawodzinski had an interesting "cyclic" theory of the development of twentieth-century Polish literature. In a German article, "Die zeitgenossische Literatur Polens," published at the same time in *Slavische Rundschau,*[2] he pointed out that while during the first decade after World War I, Polish literature was characterized by the prevalence of lyric poetry (which also invaded the domain of prose by the hypertrophy of poetic style in the trend of expressionism), the second decade brought a return to the prose form.

In his essay on Dabrowska, Zawodzinski follows the same line, giving an interesting sketch of the situation in Polish literature at the beginning of the 'thirties and then analyzing the main features of Dabrowska's prose, seeking a common denominator which would explain the enthusiastic reception given her work. This common denominator, in Zawodzinski's eyes, is her great artistic talent as an epic writer and, especially, her keen sense of realism. He does not hesitate to term Dabrowska's appearance an epoch-making event, and in his analysis of her style he promotes the view that it should be called "modernized realism":

Dabrowska's initiative on the literary level amounts—to summarize earlier remarks—to the inauguration of a new epoch in Polish literature, an epoch in which the realistic novel occupies first place. Of course, this does not mean that before her, realism had not existed in the history of the Polish novel, nor does it mean that the novel had never occupied an important place among literary genres. This was not, however, the case in the period immediately preceding the success of *Nights and Days*. It was this success which first marked the change of the aesthetic *dominant* and the literary trend which earlier had just vegetated in the background now progressed to the first plane, and this change became a fixed phenomenon in the consciousness of both readers and writers. Moreover, realism itself, which now came to the fore, was not a mere repetition of the trend which existed before; it now returned enriched, modernized, and intensified, as if it wanted to make up for its historical default.[3]

Epic elements in Dabrowska's work, and especially her ability to present ordinary characters and events so that they all breathe individualized life, are stressed by most of the critics. The term realism is of course almost always used in the more general articles and reviews of her *Nights and Days*, and it is often observed that in Dabrowska's work the traditional concept of realism based on the logic of construction gives way to a more modern concept. As mentioned, Zawodzinski calls it "modernized realism" and S. Kolaczkowski speaks of "neo-realism—a method based more on the logic of inner psychological reality than on the strictly formal logic of literary construction." [4]

This all but unanimous tone of enthusiasm that characterizes literary criticism of Dabrowska's work in the period 1922–1939 underwent a considerable change in the early postwar period when attempts at ideological re-evaluation of the entire earlier literary production were undertaken by some critics and scholars. It was especially Dabrowska's idealistic humanitarianism that be-

came the object of attacks. An example of such re-interpretation
of the ideological content of Dabrowska's work is a study by Me-
lania Kierczynska, "On People from Yonder" ("O Ludziach stamtad"), published in the policy-making *Kuznica* (No. 50, 1946).[5]
Kierczynska's main argument is not new. She elaborates, for example, on the observations made twenty years earlier by some
reviewers of *People from Yonder,* that the writer incorrectly inter-
prets the tragedies of her heroes by shifting her emphasis from
social problems to the sphere of metaphysical speculation. But
Kierczynska makes her criticism much sharper and partly denun-
ciatory by accusing Dabrowska's work of containing reactionary
associations:

We realize that a writer who tries to overcome the misery of proletarian
existence in a metaphysical way does not serve the cause of progress.[6]
The stand taken by Dabrowska is objectively in agreement with the
interest of those who profit from a system which determines the subex-
istence of the agricultural proletariat.[7]

In this quite embarrassing position, Dabrowska again found
herself paired with Joseph Conrad in serving the interests of capitalism. Thus, in defending Conrad, as she did in her *Sketches on
Conrad,* Dabrowska defended herself.

In spite of certain critical attitudes on the point of Dabrowska's
not quite "correct" interpretation of social problems, general respect and admiration for her never diminished and even such
eager Marxist critics as Kierczynska stressed the artistic values of
her work. A skillful compromise between critical and eulogistic
attitudes can be seen in the first book-length study of Dabrowska,
Wlodzimierz Maciag's *The Creative Art of Maria Dabrowska*
(*Sztuka pisarska Marii Dabrowskiej,* Cracow, 1955). The writer
is here presented as ideologically naive and passive, but artistically potent and suggestive to a degree which makes up for her
inadequacies from the point of view of Socialist Realism.

One of the most absorbing pieces of literary criticism of Dabrowska is a collection, "Four Sketches on *Nights and Days*"
("Cztery szkice o *Nocach i Dniach*") by Eva Korzeniewska, which
appeared in a book, *On Maria Dabrowska and Other Sketches* (*O*

Marii Dabrowskiej i inne szkice) by that author.[8] Korzeniewska displayed a keen sense of both formal and ideological analysis, and one must say that in spite of some oversimplifications there is a great deal of truth in her interpretation, especially of the utopian aspects of Bogumil's speculations on his position between the two social groups: landowners and working class.

Korzeniewska later edited the proceedings of the International Session in Dabrowska's honor in 1962, *Fifty Years of Maria Dabrowska's Work* (*Piecdziesiat lat tworczosci Marii Dabrowskiej*, Warsaw, 1963), where, besides the customary tributes, there are a number of significant studies. Especially notable among these are those by H. Markiewicz (on Dabrowska's novel against the background of Polish literary tradition), K. Wyka (on her literary criticism), Eva Korzeniewska (on the short stories), K. Krejči (on the problems of the "family novel," especially in comparison with Czechoslovak works of that type), Eberhard Dieckmann (on Dabrowska's travel sketches and particularly her image of Germany), Charles Hyart (on the "epic texture" of *Nights and Days*), and a few other contributions by Polish and foreign scholars.

The author of the present study has frequently quoted from materials on and by Dabrowska gathered in a useful collection, *Maria Dabrowska*, edited by Zdzislaw Libera (Warsaw, 1963). However, except for the editor's popular introduction to this work, it contains little criticism.

The most recent items of literary criticism are two popular monographs, *Maria Dabrowska*, by A. Kijowski (Warsaw, 1964) and *Noce i dnie Marii Dabrowskiej* by Tadeusz Drewnowski (Warsaw, 1965). Kijowski is not a scholar, and both his ideological and aesthetic ways are somewhat tortuous; nevertheless, he writes intelligently and interestingly, and his study is not devoid of original observations. Drewnowski's booklet is a text for high school students.

Considering the growing control over production of books, it must be noted as an important fact that Dabrowska's works have been published in huge editions.The total recently given in the weekly *Kultura* (No. 15, 1964) is 1,680,000 copies—an almost astronomical figure for Poland.

II   *Abroad*

It is interesting to see that the ideological "inadequacies" attributed to Dabrowska in Poland did not seem to bother critics in the USSR. To be sure, for them her work is foreign literature and can be viewed in the light of the different social and political reality depicted by the Polish writer. Still, the evaluation of Dabrowska's work, even in regard to her ideological interpretation of the conditions described, has often been more unreserved in the USSR than in Poland during the so-called Stalinist period.

As early as 1928, Dabrowska's collection *People from Yonder* was published in Russian (*Liudi ottuda,* translated by M. Abakina), but at that time interest in Polish literature was not very great. It increased enormously after World War II. Though Poland officially became a People's Republic, nevertheless, control of its cultural life was still far less rigid than in the Soviet Union, and its press, books, radio, and theater were attractive to the Soviet audience for their greater independence and more lively contact with Western art. One manifestation of this interest is reflected in the numerous translations from Polish. Dabrowska's stories were included in such anthologies as *The Polish Story* (*Pol'skaja novella,* Moscow, 1949) and published in periodicals like *Foreign Literature* (*Inostrannaja Literatura*). In 1955 the story, "The Village Wedding," appeared separately in a huge edition of 150,000 copies, and the comments on this story, as well as on others not yet translated at that time, were generally enthusiastic, although interpretations were usually along the lines of Socialist Realism.[9]

Finally, in 1964 the Moscow publishing house, Khudozhestvennaya Literatura, brought out *Nights and Days* (*Nochi i dni*) in the Russian translation by Eva Usievich and with an introduction by Ya. Staniukovich.

On the whole, Dabrowska's work is not yet sufficiently well known outside Poland though she is usually highly valued in foreign literary criticism. It is only natural that it is best known and most widely translated in other Slavic countries. Of the non-Slavic countries, German literature has proved the most receptive, with translations of most of Dabrowska's works and quite a few critical evaluations.

In French and English there is very little of or about Dabrow-

ska. What has been written in English is mostly of an encyclopedic nature. Thus, there is a brief passage on Dabrowska in Manfred Kridl's work, *A Survey of Polish Literature and Culture*
(New York, 1956, pp. 499–500), and also in the accompanying
Anthology of Polish Literature (New York, 1957) where an
abridged version (in Polish) of the story, "Night over the World,"
is given (pp. 594–596), preceded by a short introductory note by
L. Krzyzanowski. Kridl does not seem to have paid much attention to the structure of Dabrowska's novel, as he speaks of its
completely traditional and strictly chronological form, and repeats
such remarks by some Polish reviewers as the assertion that "it
could for that matter continue indefinitely."

A somewhat more original contribution is the observation on
Dabrowska as a short-story writer in the dissertation, *The Modern
Polish Short Story*, by Olga Scherer-Virski (Slavistic printings
and Reprintings, V, The Hague, 1955), illustrated with some fragments in Scherer-Virski's translation (pp. 233–239). The author
rightly observes Dabrowska's artistry in the delineation of character, though she is too hasty in labelling the stories as "stories of
character." She also neglects the internal unity of the collection,
calling it "a cycle with only loose connections between the works."
Of course, for her purpose it was more important to discuss each
story as a single closed unit, distinct from the point of view of the
poetics of the short story.

In the volume, *Ten Contemporary Polish Short Stories*, edited
by Edmund Ordon (Detroit, 1958), there is a good translation by
the editor of Dabrowska's "Father Philip," and it is accompanied
by remarks by Scherer-Virski (pp. xv–xvi) which summarize what
she said in her dissertation. Then there is a note by the editor of
the anthology, *The Modern Polish Mind* (Boston, 1962, p. 150),
Maria Kuncewiczowa. This is followed by a translation of the
story, "The Village Wedding" (pp. 150–171),[10] reprinted from a
volume of translations published under the same title in Poland in
1957. There is a note of approximately the same length and character in the most recent anthology, *Introduction to Modern Polish
Literature*, edited by Adam Gillon and Ludwik Krzyzanowski
(New York, 1964, p. 150), followed by a new translation of a
fragment of an unfinished novel from the war period, "On a Beautiful Summer Morning" (pp. 150–169).

Finally, an essay by the author of the present study, "Maria Dabrowska's Place in European Literature" (*Books Abroad,* Winter, 1964), is an attempt at giving the American Reader an idea of the basic ideological and aesthetic values in Dabrowska's work, and at placing her against the background of the main trends in European literature.

CHAPTER 6

In Lieu of a Conclusion

"The mystery of life, the mystery of death, the delight of human genius, the delight of human body, yes, all this we were able to grasp; but such trifles as re-shaping the world, no; this was not for us."

THIS quotation from Boris Pasternak's *Doctor Zhivago,* which summarizes the thoughts of the heroine, Lara, when she looks back on her life and her love for Zhivago, and expresses concern with problems of human life "as such" and not with problems of politics and social theories, can be applied to Maria Dabrowska as well. She once said that the most important thing for her in trying to evaluate Conrad's work was the fact that he sought to depict the "essence of human life." [1] Pasternak's concern for the imponderables of human life is somewhat the same, and Dabrowska's own striving to reach the very secret of human existence—in its relationship to other human beings—is always present in her work. From the earliest stories to her last unfinished novel, *The Adventures of a Thinking Man,* her ability to depict the miracle of the unusual, unique qualities in the ordinary, everyday existence of the most ordinary people on earth strikes the reader as the main feature of the writer's talent.

Of course, since the eternal universal theme of human destiny never ends, Dabrowska's work should always be viewed as one of the landmarks in the never ceasing development of world literature. In this treasure of works of art, works of beauty, Dabrowska's stand on the issue of literary values is on the side of artists who believe that aesthetic qualities are always intimately associated with truth and moral values. In her article, "Does Beauty Oblige?" [2] she said:

I believe in a certain amount of positive values accumulated by humanity, and in the ability to distinguish between good and evil, which is always the same. All the great writers of the world serve this moral treasure and they all agree on this basic point. The moral which can be drawn from the beauty of works written by Mann, Huxley, or Conrad, is not so much different from that which emanates from Mauriac, Tolstoy, or Dostoevsky. There exists, in spite of everything, a common language of culture and morality, and in the same way there exists a common language of beauty, a common voice of the good cause, a voice which is often neglected and forgotten but nevertheless, in its innumerable forms, perfectly understandable and acceptable for any man of good will.[3]

These are some of the basic beliefs which the writer retained all her life and which underlie all her works, both those of the early, naively enthusiastic period, and those of her latest postwar production when she was much wiser and less naive, but still persisted in her firm faith in human values.

Her epic talent developed gradually but steadily. While in the first collections of stories, idealistic beliefs and literary influence are equally strong, and account for the impression of literary exercises, her *People from Yonder* must be regarded as an accomplished work of art. Moreover, it is a work in which she even had something to contribute to the universal development of literary forms, namely the successfully executed composition of a uniformly planned volume of short stories.

Her epic talent comes fully to the fore in the novel, *Nights and Days.* In this work, the best traditional features of Realism constitute the basic element of the artistic structure, but at the same time they are masterfully replete with the most modern artistic devices blending into an individual style, rightly called "modernized Realism."

Such epic qualities in Dabrowska's work as proper distance and objectivity, and at the same time compassion and optimistic affirmation of life in its constant interplay of change and continuity must be especially stressed as important to the development of the prose form in Poland. Taken again in a wider perspective of world literature, these qualities put the Polish writer on the same level with such literary figures as Joseph Conrad or John Galsworthy in England, Thomas Mann in Germany, or Sigrid Undset in Scandinavia.

Dabrowska's affirmation of life and her unshakable faith in the indestructibility of basic human values are the most striking ideological features of her work. The writer's struggle for her ideals found an interesting echo in the unique actual life situation discussed in Chapter Four, a situation which confirmed her idealistic belief that personal values can be stronger than any political programs and affiliations. The unequalled respect Maria Dabrowska received from people in all political and ideological quarters, and the fact that even the adherents of theories alien to her heart recognized the integrity of her life and work, is perhaps the greatest tribute ever paid to a creative writer.

Notes and References

Chapter One

1. In several encyclopedic sources (and, incidentally, in this author's own essay on Dabrowska in *Books Abroad*) the date is given incorrectly as 1892.

2. In her sketch, "Warsaw of My Youth" ("Warszawa mojej młodości") Dabrowska mentions that her first attempts were submitted to *Gazeta Kaliska* when she was fifteen. Cf. *Maria Dabrowska*, ed. by Z. Libera (Warsaw, 1963), p. 103.

3. Published in *The Branch of a Cherry Tree* (*Galaz czeresni*) (Warsaw, 1922).

4. *The Misery of Wheat* was first published in a Cooperative Calendar *Spolem*, 1921, and later included in *The Branch of a Cherry Tree*.

5. *Maria Dabrowska*, ed. by Z. Libera, p. 104.

6. As can be seen from an essay on Eliza Orzeszkowa written by Dabrowska (*Pamietnik Warszawski*, No. 4, 1927).

7. It is quite fascinating to follow the strange career of this Polish writer in Germany, Scandinavia, Poland and Russia and his role as mediator of modernism. In a recent Polish study, *Polska literatura w Rosji na przelomie wieku XIX i XX* (Wroclaw, 1962) by Z. Barański, the author recalls, for example, that Przybyszewski was considered by some critics "the highest prophet and leader of the modernist movement in Russia."

8. Cf. Maria Dabrowska, *Szkice o Conradzie* (Warsaw, 1959), p. 62.

9. Cf. Jens Peter Jacobsen, *Samlede skrifter* (4th ed.; Copenhagen, 1902), II, p. 269. In her reference to Jacobsen Dabrowska quotes from her own translation.

10. The scene takes place on Christmas Eve.

11. Quoted here from Maria Dabrowska, *Opowiadania* (Cracow, n.d.), pp. 182–83.

12. For a detailed discussion of these problems, see my work, *La*

fonction des éléments dialectaux dans les oeuvres littéraires (Uppsala, 1949).

13. *Opowiadania,* p. 57.

14. A precise stylistic analysis on the basis of translation is almost impossible. To illustrate the point of mixing linguistic levels, the quoted Polish examples, *jest, jes, je* could perhaps be compared to the English expressions, *you are, you're, you is;* all in the speech of the same person.

15. See the essay, "Maria Dabrowska. Historyczne-literackie znaczenie jej tworczosci" in K. W. Zawodzinski; *Opowiesci o powiesci* (Cracow, 1963), p. 270.

16. *Opowiadania,* p. 160.

17. *Ibid.,* p. 183.

Chapter Two

1. See Ford Madox Ford, *Joseph Conrad. A Personal Remembrance* (London, 1924), p. 204.

2. The most publicized attempts in this respect are the much more recent experiments by the French trio: Michel Butor, Alain Robbe-Grillet and Natalie Sarraute. But actually quite a few earlier examples of these anti-genre attitudes could be quoted. In analyzing C. K. Norwid's artistic prose, I found the term "anti-short story form," *avant la lettre,* applicable to Norwid's peculiar *White Flowers.* Cf. Z. Folejewski, "C. K. Norwid and the Poetics of the Short Story," *American Contributions to the Fifth International Congress of Slavists in Sofia* (The Hague, 1964).

3. Cf. Boris Eikhenbaum, "O'Henry i teoriya novelly," *Zvezda,* No. 6 (June, 1925), p. 292.

4. See *Wspolczesna powiesc polska* (Warsaw, p. 906), p. 11.

5. Quoted here from *Maria Dabrowska,* ed. by Z. Libera, p. 115.

6. *Ibid.*

7. *Kultura,* No. 5, 1931.

8. See Henryk Markiewicz, "*Noce i Dnie* na tle polskiej tradycji powiesciowej." *Piecdziesiat lat tworczosci Marii Dabrowskiej,* ed. by Ewa Korzeniewska (Warsaw, 1963), p. 34.

9. "O typowosci w literaturze polskiej." *Pamietnik Literacki,* XLVIII, 1957, pp. 46–82.

10. Maria Dabrowska, *Noce i dnie,* Part IV (Warsaw, 1934), II, pp. 158–59.

11. *Ibid.,* p. 159.

12. See *Maria Dabrowska,* ed. by Z. Libera, pp. 119–20.

13. *Noce i dnie,* Part IV, II, pp. 119–20.

14. See *Maria Dabrowska,* ed. by Z. Libera, p. 120.

Notes and References

15. *Ibid.*
16. *Noce i dnie,* Part IV, II, p. 335.
17. From this point of view, it would be of some interest to compare Dabrowska's novel to a Swedish family cycle written at exactly the same time by Agnes von Krusenstjerna, *The Misses von Pahlen* (*Fröknarna von Pahlen*), published in seven volumes in Stockholm in the early thirties, where sexual, homosexual, and heterosexual experiences may seem to be the main preoccupation.
18. See Maria Dabrowska, *Szkice o Conradzie* (Warsaw, 1959), p. 77.
19. Cf. Joseph Conrad, *Nostromo* (New York, 1926) p. 318. (Dabrowska quotes from the Polish translation.)
20. *Szkice o Conradzie,* p. 77.
21. See *Rozdroze,* p. 108.
22. *Noce i dnie,* Part IV, II, pp. 190–91.
23. *Ibid.,* pp. 198–200.
24. See *Maria Dabrowska,* ed. by Z. Libera, p. 118.

Chapter Three

1. See *Maria Dabrowska,* ed. by Z. Libera, p. 116.
2. In her Introduction to the second edition of *People from Yonder* (Warsaw, 1935); quoted here from the sixth edition (Cracow, 1945), p. 11.
3. See Conrad's letter to Edward Garnett of July 14, 1923 in Joseph Conrad, *Letters to Edward Garnett* (London, 1928).
4. See, M. B. Orvis, *Short Story Writing* (New York, 1928), pp. 74–75, and W. F. Wright, *Romance and Tragedy in Joseph Conrad* (Lincoln, Nebraska, 1949), p. 27.
5. See *Maria Dabrowska,* ed. by Z. Libera, p. 127.
6. *O Marii Dabrowskiej i inne szkice* (Wroclaw, 1956).
7. *Ibid.,* pp. 15–16.
8. See Julian Przybos, Speech at the Jubilee of Maria Dabrowska, in *Piecdziesiat lat tworczosci Marii Dabrowskiej, pp.* 23–24.
9. See *Maria Dabrowska,* ed. by Z. Libera, p. 118.
10. Quoted here from K. W. Zawodzinski, *Opowiesci o powiesci* (Cracow, 1963), p. 270.
11. Joseph Conrad, *The Short Tales* (New York, 1924), p. ix.
12. See *Noce i Dnie,* Part I, I, pp. 33–36.
13. *Ibid.,* Part I, II, pp. 379–80.
14. *Noce i dnie,* Part I, II, pp. 265–66. Here, again, it is impossible to reproduce the exact stylistic quality, which is based on an untranslatable, non-idiomatic usage of words by the speaker (*ono jest w samo prawie*).

15. Cf. Chapter Two, note 12.
16. *Noce i dnie,* Part I, II, p. 297.
17. *Ibid.,* Part I, II, p. 63.
18. *Ibid.,* Part I, II, p. 352.
19. *Ibid.,* Part III, pp. 35–36.
20. See Thomas Mann, *Buddenbrooks* (London, 1941), p. 38.

Chapter Four

1. Quoted from *Ten Contemporary Polish Stories,* ed. by E. Orden (Detroit, 1958), pp. 33–34.
2. Dabrowska translated several stories for the two-volume selection of Anton Chekhov's works, *Utwory wybrane,* which appeared in Warsaw in 1953.
3. See *Piecdziesiat lat tworczosci Marii Dabrowskiej,* ed. by E. Korzeniewska (Wroclaw, 1956), pp. 121–122.
4. See *Maria Dabrowska,* ed. by Z. Libera, p. 163. Since the reference to "our contemporary Jan Zamoyski" could have been construed to be an allusion to J. Pilsudski, the passage (and, indeed, the whole article) required a good deal of civil courage on the part of the writer. Any real or alleged unfavorable reference to Pilsudski at that time could be regarded as *crimen laesae maiestatis.*
5. For further details see Z. Folejewski, "Socialist Realism in Polish Literature and Criticism," *Comparative Literature,* XIII, pp. 72–81.
6. The popular device of writing novels on themes from the more or less distant past, practiced at the time by many Polish writers, was regarded as escapism.
7. See *Mysli o sprawach i ludziach* (Warsaw, 1956), pp. 140–141. When writing the preface to this volume in 1956, Dabrowska felt obliged to stress the fact that her criticism of certain "deficiencies in cultural policy in Poland" were in specific reference to the period before 1956. She pointed out, however, that she came to the conclusion that "a few words of caution and a few definitions which it is good to keep in mind" should not remain unsaid" (*Ibid.,* p. 7).
8. The term, "Deluge" in Polish history refers to the series of devastating wars in the 17th century when Polish territories were invaded by several foreign armies. Szczotka's study refers specifically to the Swedish invasion.
9. *Mysli o sprawach i ludziach,* pp. 41–42.
10. See *Gwiazda Zaranna,* p. 13.
11. *Ibid.,* p. 14.
12. *Ibid.,* p. 24.
13. *Ibid.,* p. 15.

14. Quoted here from Maria Dabrowska, *Szkice o Conradzie,* pp. 164–165.

15. *Gwiazda Zaranna,* p. 96.

16. Cf., for example, a review article on *Gwiazda Zaranna* in the Polish émigré weekly, *Wiadomosci,* No. 20 (London, 1956).

17. See *Szkice o Conradzie,* pp. 159–160.

18. In Dabrowska's life this incident constitutes a thematic rhyme of a kind, which echoes a situation mentioned earlier in this book, when Dabrowska as a young woman, at the beginning of her literary career, stood up to the ruling group in protest against the imprisonment of the opponents of Pilsudski's regime.

Chapter Five

1. Vol. 43, 1933, No. 129, pp. 49–60, and No. 130, pp. 222–40; also in offprint, Cracow, 1933. Quoted here from the posthumous volume of Zawodzinski's essays on prose, *Opowiesci o powiesci,* ed. by C. Zgorzelski (Cracow, 1963), pp. 256–86.

2. No. 5, 1933, pp. 230–42.

3. *Opowiesci o powiesci,* p. 290.

4. Cf. S. Kolaczkowski, "Literatura polska 1932," *Rocznik Literacki* for 1932 (Warsaw, 1933), p. 15.

5. Later re-published in a textbook for teachers' colleges, *Materialy do nauczania historii literatury polskiej* (Warsaw, 1950), II, pp. 131–139.

6. Quoted here from *Materialy do nauczania historii literatury polskiej,* p. 134.

7. *Ibid.,* p. 139.

8. *Studia Historyczno Literackie,* Polska Akademia Nauk. Instytut Badan Literackich, vol. XXX (Wroclaw, 1956).

9. Cf., for example, "Under the Banner of Struggle for Socialist Realism" ("Pod znakom borby za sotsjalisticheskij realizm"), *Pravda,* No. 73, 1956.

10. Still another fragment ("A Happy Creature," pp. 389–400) is given in this anthology as an example (not very well chosen, to be sure) of "Polish humor."

Chapter Six

1. See Dabrowska's essay, "Spotkanie z Conradem w podrozy," *Pion,* 1934. Quoted here from *Szkice o Conradzie,* p. 109.

2. "Czy piekno zobowiazuje," *Pion,* 1935.

3. Quoted here from *Maria Dabrowska,* ed. by Z. Libera, p. 67.

Selected Bibliography

PRIMARY SOURCES

Galaz czeresni (*The Branch of a Cherry Tree*). Warsaw: Zwiazek Polskich Stowarzyszen Spozywcow, 1922.

Usmiech dziecinstwa (*The Smile of Childhood*). Warsaw: Towarzystwo Wydawnicze, 1923.

Ludzie stamtad (*People from Yonder*). Warsaw: J. Mortkowicz, 1926.

Noce i dnie (*Nights and Days*); Part I, *Bogumil i Barbara* (*Bogumil and Barbara*). Warsaw: J. Mortkowicz, 1932.

Noce i dnie; Part II, *Wieczne zmartwienie* (*Eternal Worry*). Warsaw: J. Mortkowicz, 1932.

Noce i dnie; Part III, *Milosc* (*Love*). Warsaw: J. Mortkowicz, 1933. 2 vols.

Noce i dnie; Part IV, *Wiatr w oczy* (*Wind in the Eyes*). Warsaw: J. Mortkowicz, 1934. 2 vols.

Znaki zycia (*Signs of Life*). Warsaw: J. Mortkowicz, 1938.

Geniusz sierocy (*Orphan Genius*). Warsaw: J. Mortkowicz, 1938.

Stanislaw i Bogumil (*Stanislaw and Bogumil*). Warsaw: E. Kuthan, 1948.

Gwiazda zaranna (*The Morning Star*). Warsaw: Czytelnik, 1955.

Mysli o sprawach i ludziach (*Thoughts on Problems and People*). Warsaw: Czytelnik, 1956.

Pisma wybrane (*Selected Works*). Warsaw: Czytelnik, 1956. 3 vols.

Dramaty (*Dramatic Works*). Warsaw: Panstwowy Inst. Wydawniczy, 1957.

Szkice o Conradzie (*Sketches on Conrad*). Warsaw: Panstwowy Inst. Wydawniczy, 1959.

Przygody czlowieka myslacego (*Adventures of a Thinking Man*). Serialized novel: *Przeglad Kulturalny*, 1961–1963.

Pisma rozproszone (*Scattered Works*). Edited by Ewa Korzeniewska. Cracow: Wydawnictwo Literackie, 1964. 2 vols.

SECONDARY SOURCES

ADAMCZEWSKI, STANISLAW, "Wielkie dzielo Marii Dabrowskiej," *Kultura*, 1932. Contains interesting remarks on the ideological aspects of *Nights and Days* and on Dabrowska's skill in psychological analysis.

DREWNOWSKI, TADEUSZ, *Noce i Dnie Marii Dabrowskiej*. Warsaw: Panstwowe Zaklady Wydawnictw Szkolnych, 1965. Text for high schools.

FOLEJEWSKI, ZBIGNIEW. "Maria Dabrowska's Place in European Literature," *Books Abroad*, (Winter, 1964). Brief introduction to the main aspects of Dabrowska's literary work.

KIJOWSKI, ANDRZEJ. *Maria Dabrowska*. Warsaw: Wiedza Powszechna, 1964. A general synthetic presentation of popular character.

KORZENIEWSKA, EWA. *O Marii Dabrowskiej i inne szkice*. Wroclaw: Ossolineum, 1956. A thorough though somewhat one-sided analysis of ideological and stylistic aspects of Dabrowska's work.

KORZENIEWSKA, EWA. ed. *Piecdziesiat lat tworczosci Marii Dabrowskiej*. Warsaw: Panstwowy Instytut Wydawniczy, 1964. Proceedings of the Scholarly Session in Dabrowska's Honor in Warsaw and Kalisz under the auspices of the Polish Academy. Articles by various hands on different aspects of Dabrowska's work and its reception outside of Poland. Also bibliography.

KRIDL, MANFRED. *A Survey of Polish Literature and Culture*. New York: Columbia University Press, 1956. A brief information of encyclopedic character.

LIBERA, ZDZISLAW. ed. *Maria Dabrowska*. Warsaw: Panstwowe Zaklady Wyd. Szkolnych, 1963. Brief sketch of Dabrowska's life and excerpts of the writer's own and others' comments on her work.

MACIAG, WLODZIMIERZ. *Sztuka pisarska Marii Dabrowskiej*. Cracow: Wydawnictwo Literackie, 1955. First book-length study of Dabrowska's works. Mostly traditional and biographical in approach. The ideological analysis follows the line of Socialist Realism.

PIWINSKI, LEON. "Noce i dnie. Uwagi o pierwszych dwoch tomach powiesci Marii Dabrowskiej," *Wiadomosci Literackie*, VII, 1933. Penetrating remarks on *Nights and Days*.

SCHERER-VIRSKI, OLGA. *The Modern Polish Short Story*. The Hague: Mouton, 1955. A discussion of Dabrowska's short-story techniques.

WYKA, KAZIMIERZ. "Czas i czlowiek w *Nocach i dniach*," *Kultura*, XIX, 1932. A good, concise analysis of *Nights and Days* as an epic work.

ZAWODZINSKI, KAROL W. "Maria Dabrowska: Historyczno-literackie znaczenie jej tworczosci," *Przyglad Wspolczesny*, XLIV, 1933

(Separate edition, Cracow, 1933). The first substantial study, with a number of important remarks on Dabrowska's epic talent and her place in literature.

For bibliography of M. Dabrowska's fiction, stories, articles, criticism, first editions, and translations, check *Maria Dabrowska*, ed. by Z. Libera, pp. 326–332, and *Piecdziesiat lat tworczosci Marii Dabrowskiej*, ed. by E. Korzeniewska, pp. 339–374. Also: *Slownik Wspolczesnych pisarzy polskich* (Warsaw: Panstwowe Wyd. Naukowe, 1963), I, pp. 409–419.

Index

Names of characters in Dabrowska's works are followed by the title
—in parentheses—of the book in which they appear.

Index

[121]

Index